Mary E

Engaging God's Word

Acts

Judge

Engage Bible Studies

Tools That Transform

Engage Bible Studies

an imprint of

 COMMUNITY BIBLE STUDY

Engaging God's Word: Acts
Copyright © 2012 by Community Bible Study. All rights reserved.
ISBN 978-1-62194-015-9

Published by Community Bible Study
790 Stout Road
Colorado Springs, CO
1-800-826-4181
www.communitybiblestudy.org

Printed in the United States of America.

Contents

Introduction

Welcome to the life-changing adventure of engaging with God's Word! Whether this is the first time you've opened a Bible or you've studied the Scriptures all your life, good things are in store for you. Studying the Bible is unlike any other kind of study you have ever done. That's because the Word of God is *"living and active"* (Hebrews 4:12) and transcends time and cultures. The earth and heavens as we know them will one day pass away, but God's Word never will (Mark 13:31). It's as relevant to your life today as it was to the people who wrote it down centuries ago. And the fact that God's Word is living and active means that reading God's Word is always meant to be a personal experience. God's Word is not just dead words on a page—it is page after page of living, powerful words—so get ready, because the time you spend studying the Bible in this *Engaging God's Word* course will be life-transforming!

Why Study the Bible?

Some Christians read the Bible because they know they're supposed to. It's a good thing to do, and God expects it. And all that's true! However, there are many additional reasons to study God's Word. Here are just some of them.

We get to know God through His Word. Our God is a relational God who knows us and wants us to know Him. The Scriptures, which He authored, reveal much about Him: how He thinks and feels, what His purposes are, what He thinks about us, how He views the world He made, what He has planned for the future. The Bible shows us God's many attributes—His kindness, goodness, justice, love, faithfulness, mercy, compassion, creativity, redemption, sovereignty, and so on. As we get to know Him through His Word, we come to love and trust Him.

God speaks to us through His Word. One of the primary ways God speaks to us is through His written Word. Don't be surprised if, as you read the Bible, certain parts nearly jump off the page at you, almost as if they'd been written with you in mind. God is the Author of this incredible book, so that's not just possible, it's likely! Whether it is to find comfort, warning, correction, teaching, or guidance, always approach God's Word with your spiritual ears open (Isaiah 55:3) because God, your loving heavenly Father, has things He wants to say to you.

God's Word brings life. Just about everyone wants to learn the secret to "the good life." And the good news is, that secret is found in God's Word. Don't think of the Bible as a bunch of rules. Viewing it with that mindset is a distortion. God gave us His Word because as our Creator and the Creator of the universe, He alone knows how life was meant to work. He knows that love makes us happier than hate, that generosity brings more joy than greed, and that integrity allows us to rest more peacefully at night than deception does. God's ways are not always "easiest" but they are the way to life. As the Psalmist says, *"If Your law had not been my delight, I would have perished in my affliction. I will never forget Your precepts, for by them You have given me life"* (Psalm 119:92-93).

God's Word offers stability in an unstable world. Truth is an ever-changing negotiable for many people in our culture today. But building your life on constantly changing "truth" is like building your house on shifting sand. God's Word, like God Himself, never changes. What He says was true yesterday, is true today, and will still be true a billion years from now. Jesus said, *"Everyone then who hears these words of Mine and does them will be like a wise man who built his house on the rock"* (Matthew 7:24).

God's Word helps us to pray effectively. When we read God's Word and get to know what He is really like, we understand better how to pray. God answers prayers that are according to His will. We discover His will by reading the Bible. First John 5:14-15 tells us that *"this is the confidence that we have toward Him, that if we ask anything according to His will He hears us. And if we know that He hears us in whatever we ask, we know that we have the requests that we have asked of Him."*

How to Get the Most out of *Engaging God's Word*

Each *Engaging God's Word* study contains key elements that have been carefully designed to help you get the most out of your time in God's Word. Slightly modified for your study-at-home success, this approach is very similar to the tried-and-proven Bible study method that Community Bible Study has used with thousands of men, women, and children across the United States and around the world for nearly 40 years. There are some basic things you can expect to find in each course in this series.

- ❖ Lesson 1 provides an overview of the Bible book (or books) you will study and questions to help you focus, anticipate, and pray about what you will be learning.

- ❖ Every lesson contains questions to answer on your own, commentary that reviews and clarifies the passage, and three special sections called "Apply what you have learned," "Think about" and "Personalize this lesson."

- ❖ Some lessons contain memory verse suggestions.

Whether you plan to use *Engaging God's Word* on your own or with a group, here are some suggestions that will help you enjoy and receive the most benefit from your study.

Spread out each lesson over several days. Your *Engaging God's Word* lessons were designed to take a week to complete. Spreading out your study rather than doing it all at once allows time for the things God is teaching you to sink in and for you to practice applying them.

Pray each time you read God's Word. The Bible is a book unlike any other because God Himself inspired it. The same Spirit who inspired the human authors who wrote it will help you to understand and apply it if you ask Him to. So make it a practice to ask Him to make His Word come alive to you every time you read it.

Read the whole passage covered in the lesson. Before plunging into the questions, take time to read the specific chapter or verses that will be covered in that lesson. Doing this will give you important context for the whole lesson. Reading the Bible in context is an important principle in interpreting it accurately.

Begin learning the memory verse. Learning Scripture by heart requires discipline, but the rewards far outweigh the effort. Memorizing a verse allows you to recall it whenever you need it—for personal encouragement and direction, or to share with someone else. Consider writing the verse on a sticky note or index card that you can post where you will see it often or carry with you to review during the day. Reading and re-reading the verse often—out loud when possible—is a simple way to commit it to memory.

Re-read the passage for each section of questions. Each lesson is divided into sections so that you study one small part of Scripture at a time. Before attempting to answer the questions, review the verses that the questions will cover.

Answer the questions without consulting the Commentary or other reference materials. There is great joy in having the Holy Spirit teach you God's Word on your own, without the help of outside resources. Don't cheat yourself of the delight of discovery by reading the Commentary prematurely. Wait until after you've completed the lesson.

Repeat the process for all the question sections.

Prayerfully consider the "Apply what you have learned," marked with the 📌 push pin symbol. The vision of Community Bible Study is not to just gain knowledge about the Bible, but to be transformed by it. For this reason, each set of questions closes with a section that encourages you to apply what you are learning. Usually this section involves action—something for you to do. As you practice these suggestions, your life will change.

Read the Commentary. *Engaging God's Word* commentaries are written by theologians whose goal is to help you understand the context of what you are studying as it relates to the rest of Scripture, God's character, and what the passage means for your life. Of necessity, the commentaries include the author's interpretations. While interesting and helpful, keep in mind that the Commentary is simply one person's understanding of what these passages mean. Other godly men and women have views that are also worth considering.

Pause to contemplate each "Think about" section, marked with the notepad symbol. These features, embedded in the Commentary, offer a place to pause and consider some of the principles being brought out by the text. They provide excellent ideas to journal about or to discuss with other believers, especially those doing the study with you.

Jot down insights or prayer points from the "Personalize this lesson" marked with the ☑ check box symbol. While the "Apply what you have learned" section focuses on doing, the "Personalize this lesson" section focuses on becoming. Spiritual transformation is not just about doing right things and refraining from doing wrong things—it is about changing from the inside out. To be transformed means letting God change our hearts so that our attitudes, emotions, desires, reactions, and goals are increasingly like Jesus'. Often this section will discuss something that you cannot do in your own strength—so your response will usually be something to pray about. Remember that becoming more Christ-like is not just a matter of trying harder—it requires God's empowerment.

The Birth of Christianity

The Acts of the Apostles chronicles the birth and growth of the early church. This exciting narrative is filled with signs and wonders, danger, conflict, and testimonies to the gospel of Christ. It begins with Christ's ascension and ends with the apostle Paul living as a prisoner in Rome.

Acts gives us an extensive cast of characters. Central to this story are the apostles, primarily Peter and Paul. We see Peter taking charge in the leadership of the early church, speaking out boldly about Jesus, being jailed and miraculously freed, and becoming an advocate for Gentile believers following a vision from God. We also meet Paul (formerly Saul), a persecutor of the church, who becomes a believer after Jesus appears to him on the road to Emmaus. The church commissions Paul to take missionary journeys to spread the gospel throughout the region. Though he longs to see the Jews know Jesus, Paul becomes the apostle to the Gentiles, planting and encouraging young churches wherever he goes, despite continual hardship and opposition.

In Acts we also see the early days of the church. As the apostles preach about the risen Savior, thousands believe and are baptized. The early believers are devoted to teaching and fellowship, and gladly pool their resources so that no one is in need. When conflict arises over whether non-Jewish believers should have to follow Jewish laws, the church in Jerusalem holds a council and comes to a decision respecting both sides.

The Jews figure prominently in the story. While some believe, many Jewish leaders are enraged by the apostles' teaching. They continually try to suppress the Christian movement, even attempting to have Paul killed on numerous occasions.

Finally, we see the occupying Roman leaders become involved as civil unrest rises up around the preaching of the gospel. Some offer objective judgments and protect the apostles; others pander to the Jews' wishes and impede the missionaries' work.

Themes in Acts include

❖ the important role of the Holy Spirit in the birth of the church and the spread of the gospel

❖ the importance of the Resurrection in the gospel message

❖ God's inclusion of non-Jews in the family of believers

❖ persecution and suffering as a part of preaching Christ

1. As you begin this study, what questions do you have about the early days of the church?

    _____

    _____

2. What questions do you have about the Holy Spirit?

    _____

    _____

3. What would you like to learn about being a witness for Christ?

    _____

    _____

4. How would you summarize your goals for completing this study of Acts?

    _____

    _____

If you are doing this study with a group, listen to one another's answers to the questions above. Share the areas in which you would like to learn or grow, and pray for one another about what you share. If you are doing this study alone, talk with God about what you hope to receive from Him over the course of this study.

The Birth of Christianity

The Acts of the Apostles is a communication between two friends. Addressed to a Greek named Theophilus, a sophisticated and well-educated man, Acts is an account of the beginnings of Christianity. Having already received Luke's Gospel account regarding what *"Jesus began to do and to teach"* (Acts 1:1), Theophilus receives Acts, the continuation of the Gospel narrative.

The Author

Nearly universal consensus supports the Gospel writer Luke as the author of this book as well. Church tradition holds that Luke was a Gentile. If so, Luke is the only non-Jewish writer of the Bible. Luke was a companion and co-worker of the apostle Paul, as well as a doctor. In both the Gospel of Luke and Acts, Luke uses medical terminology to describe ailments and cures. Both writings show concern for the sick and compassion for the poor. The two accounts display an almost identical literary style. Together they make up one continuous, well-planned narrative of Christ's teachings and the early days of the Christian church.

Think about the scope of God's love shown throughout the Bible. In the Old Testament, we see God's love revealed primarily to the Jews, but even at that time He intended for all people to receive His mercy. Isaiah declared to God's people that they were to be His witnesses, showing the way of salvation to the world: *"I will make you as a light for the nations, that my salvation may reach to the end of the earth"* (Isaiah 49:6). In Acts, God demonstrates His acceptance of all people on the basis of their faith in Christ.

The Pattern

Acts shows the expansion of Christianity from its beginnings in the
Holy City of the Hebrews, Jerusalem, to the capital city of the Gentiles,
Rome. The gospel's journey to Rome does not progress in a straight line;
it follows an irregular course from Jerusalem to Damascus, Antioch, Asia
Minor, Macedonia, Greece, and back to Jerusalem many times.

 Think about the Holy Spirit's role in establishing
the Church. Without the constant guidance and
empowerment of the Holy Spirit, the apostles would
not have been able to spread the gospel effectively.
Acts shows the Holy Spirit being poured out upon believers,
along with numerous instances of Jews and Gentiles
receiving the Spirit following the initial outpouring at
Pentecost (Acts 8:16; 9:17; 10:44).

Structural Features

Luke organizes his account to show how the scope of witnessing for
Christ broadens. The 12 apostles witness to Jews in Jerusalem (1:1-5:42);
then seven disciples witness to Hellenists and Samaritans (6:1-9:31);
and finally, Peter and Paul witness to Gentiles (9:32-28:31). The book
can be divided into nine sections, each closing with a "progress report":
"The Lord added to their number day by day those who were being saved"
(1:1-2:47). *"More than ever believers were added to the Lord, multitudes of
both men and women"* (3:1-5:14). *"The word of God continued to increase, ...
and a great many of the priests became obedient to the faith"* (5:17-6:7). *"The
church throughout all Judea and Galilee and Samaria had peace and was
being built up"* (6:8-9:31). *"The hand of the Lord was with them, and a great
number who believed turned to the Lord"* (10:1-11:21). *"The word of God
increased and multiplied"* (11:22-12:24). *"The churches were strengthened
in the faith, and they increased in numbers daily"* (13:1-16:5). *"The word of
the Lord continued to increase and prevail mightily"* (16:6-19:20). *"[Paul]
lived there two whole years ... proclaiming the kingdom of God and teaching
about the Lord Jesus Christ with all boldness and without hindrance"* (19:21-
28:31). In addition, Luke records the speeches of 1st-century leaders,
including Peter, Paul, Stephen, Gamaliel, James, the town clerk at

Ephesus, Tertullus, and Festus. These sermons and speeches help to break up the narrative and add interest.

Luke's Objectives in Writing Acts

From studying Acts, we can see six objectives Luke may have had in writing this book:

- ❖ To describe the growth of the Christian church as prophesied by the risen Christ before His ascension.
- ❖ To highlight the gospel's worldwide spread among many different cultures. Luke shows how the gospel of Christ was preached among the Jews and to an increasing number of Gentiles.
- ❖ To present Peter and Paul as leaders with equal authority in the early church. The Jews tend to look to Peter as their authority, the Gentiles to Paul.
- ❖ To serve as an instrument to commend Christianity to the Roman government, citing cases where Roman officials speak well of believers.
- ❖ To show that Jesus' suffering, death, and resurrection; the creation of the church; Paul's conversion; and the inclusion of the Gentiles all took place to fulfill Scripture.
- ❖ To emphasize that Christ's followers will not escape suffering and harassment, but faith and the power of the Holy Spirit enable believers to continue Jesus' preaching, teaching, and healing ministry.

The Surprising Conclusion

In a book so full of miracles and accounts of the Holy Spirit's work in the world, we might expect a climactic ending. However, Acts ends abruptly, like an unfinished narrative. Luke's ending may or may not have been intentional. Perhaps he was unable to continue recording Paul's missionary work, or he may have meant to leave the book open-ended, as the account of the history of the church is still being written.

Believers today are participating in the ongoing history of the church and will continue to do so as long as souls can be won for God's kingdom, or until Jesus comes again. Our calling is to continue spreading the good news.

Personalize this lesson.

The miraculous growth of the church happened by the work of the Holy Spirit through the changed lives of believers. When we have been freed from sin through faith in the Son of God, we no longer need to be driven by our earthly goals or to find satisfaction for our earthly needs. How we choose to live our lives can show others that Christ is real.

Think about how Jesus has changed your life—either when you came to know Him, or gradually, over time, as you have grown spiritually. How are you different from what you might have been without knowing Christ? Spend some time thanking God for the new person you are in Christ. Ask Him to give you an opportunity this week to tell an unbeliever about what He has done for and in you.

The Promise
Acts 1

Memorize God's Word: Acts 1:8.

❖ Acts 1:1-5—Introduction

1. Read Luke 1:1-4. What do you learn about Luke's personality?

    _____

    _____

    _____

2. Based on Luke's introduction to the Gospel of Luke (Luke 1:1-4), what might you expect about the book of Acts?

    _____

    _____

    _____

3. In Acts 1:3, Luke refers to *"many proofs"* of Jesus' resurrection. Read the following passages and record the evidence in each account.

    a. Luke 24:1-12 _____

    _____

    _____

    b. John 20:19-29 _____

    _____

    _____

❖ Acts 1:6-8—Jesus' Promise of the Holy Spirit

4. What might the apostles be thinking when they ask the question in verse 6?

    _____

    _____

5. Based on His response to their question, what is Jesus trying to do?

    _____

    _____

    _____

6. Verse 8 states the theme of the book of Acts. In your own words, what is this theme?

    _____

    _____

    _____

7. Referring to 1 John 1:1-4, how would you define the word *witness*?

    _____

    _____

8. On the basis of this verse and Acts 1:8, to whom do we witness?

    _____

    _____

9. What promise do you find in verse 8?

    _____

    _____

10. Why do you think God chooses to give people the privilege and responsibility of witnessing to others?

    _____

    _____

    _____

❖ Acts 1:9-11—Christ Ascends Into Heaven

11. What had to happen before Jesus could send the Holy Spirit to empower believers (John 7:39)?

_____

_____

12. According to the following verses, what is the significance of the Ascension?

a. Romans 8:34 _____

_____

b. Ephesians 1:15-23 _____

_____

_____

❖ Acts 1:12-26—The Apostles Meet in the Upper Room

13. What is the attitude of the believers gathered in the upper room?

_____

_____

14. What might they have been praying for?

_____

_____

15. Judas was one of the original apostles, chosen by Christ Himself. Considering 2 Peter 3:9, what did Jesus hope for after Judas's betrayal?

_____

_____

16. What requirement is necessary for Judas's replacement (Acts 1:21-22)?

_____

_____

17. Why do you think this requirement was necessary?

_____

_____

18. According to 1 Corinthians 15:17, what is the significance of
    Jesus' resurrection to the Christian faith?

_____

_____

_____

Apply what you have learned. God promises
to give us the Holy Spirit's power to tell others
about Jesus. Envision yourself sharing the gospel
with someone you know. Why is God's promise of power
for witnessing so important? Think of several friends,
acquaintances, or family members who do not know the
Lord. Thank God for His promise to give you power as you
witness to each one.

The Promise
Acts 1

Acts is the only biblical record of the early days of Christianity. Paul's letters contain scattered fragments of information, but only the book of Acts gives an organized, cohesive account of the development of the early Christian church. Luke had already written to his friend and fellow Greek, Theophilus, about Jesus and His ministry and is eager to continue his narrative to enrich his friend's spiritual knowledge.

Days of Expectation

During the 40 days between Jesus' resurrection and ascension, He appears to His followers and teaches them *"about the Kingdom of God"* (Acts 1:3). These encounters with the risen Lord restore confidence to the disciples, who have been frightened since the Crucifixion by what Jesus' enemies might do to them. At this time, the Lord commands His followers not to leave Jerusalem until they receive the gift His Father has promised them—baptism with the Holy Spirit.

Before the Holy Spirit was sent to His followers, Jesus could only be in one place at a time. This limitation is overcome when His followers are *"clothed with power from on high"* (Luke 24:49). As a result of the Holy Spirit descending to indwell His disciples at Pentecost, Jesus' ministry would operate in many different places at the same time and through many different people.

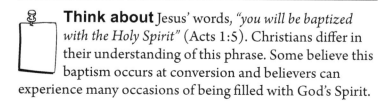

Think about Jesus' words, *"you will be baptized with the Holy Spirit"* (Acts 1:5). Christians differ in their understanding of this phrase. Some believe this baptism occurs at conversion and believers can experience many occasions of being filled with God's Spirit.

Others believe baptism of the Spirit is distinct and separate from conversion. They hold that believers are indwelt and sealed by God's Spirit at conversion and are then, or on a different occasion, filled with the Holy Spirit, an experience that often involves the person speaking in tongues. Some Christians believe that speaking in tongues is limited to the apostolic age and does not occur today. Regardless of our differences about this baptism, we can all be grateful for the Holy Spirit, who unifies all believers in Christ and makes us effective witnesses.

The Task Clarified

Jesus answers many of the disciples' questions, but they remain puzzled by His teachings on God's kingdom. The disciples ask Him, *"Lord, will You at this time restore the kingdom to Israel?"* (1:6), to which He replies, *"It is not for you to know times or seasons that the Father has fixed by His own authority"* (1:7).

To the Jews, restoring the kingdom to Israel meant reestablishing Israel as a world political power with a leader who would rival Caesar. They believed that Jesus had such power—after all, He conquered death—and that they would share in His earthly rule. Jesus explains that the kingdom He speaks of is not an earthly one. He tells them, *"You will receive power when the Holy Spirit has come on you, and you will be My witnesses in Jerusalem and in all Judea and Samaria, and to the end of the earth"* (1:8). Once equipped with the Holy Spirit, the disciples are to leave Jerusalem (the capital city of Israel) to travel to Judea (the surrounding countryside), then north to the despised Samaritans, and finally to *"the end of the earth."* Instead of political positions, the disciples will be given spiritual power to spread the good news of the gospel to the world.

 Think about what it means to be a witness for the Lord. Others see the grace and power of Christ through our words, actions, and attitudes. How does your life give a positive witness for the Lord?

The Ascension

After Jesus disappears from sight, two angels appear and tell the disciples that He has returned to heaven. Now at God's right hand, Jesus is restored to the position of glory He had with the Father before His incarnation. The angels tell the disciples, *"Jesus ... will come in the same way as you saw Him go into heaven"* (Acts 1:11). The messengers are referring to the Second Coming, Christ's return to earth to establish His kingdom at the end of the age.

Return to Headquarters

After Jesus' ascension, His followers, whom Luke lists by name in 1:13, go directly to an upper room to wait and pray. This room may have been where Jesus celebrated His final meal with the disciples or a room in the home of John Mark's mother. With the group are women who were devoted to Jesus during His lifetime, including His mother, Mary, and possibly the sisters and wives of the 11 disciples. Jesus' brothers are there as well. The group spends days in prayer.

Peter and the Twelve

Soon after the Ascension, Peter emerges as the leader of the 11 disciples and the larger group of 120 believers who are to receive the Holy Spirit on the day of Pentecost. Peter speaks to the group of the many recent events that have happened as fulfillment of Scripture, including Judas Iscariot's treachery, prophesized in Psalm 69:25. The description of Judas's death in Luke 1:18-19 is likely not part of Peter's original message. Perhaps Luke includes it only for the benefit of Theophilus. Enclosing the passage in parentheses supports this idea.

Choosing Matthias

Peter believes the 12th position among the disciples that had been occupied by Judas should be filled, particularly by one who observed Jesus' ministry from the time of His baptism to the Ascension. Peter asks the group to nominate and choose a replacement for Judas. Two men are nominated. After praying, the group members cast lots, and Matthias is chosen as the new disciple. Casting lots was a method used in the Old Testament to discern God's will. Proverbs 16:33 states: *"The lot is cast into the lap, but its every decision is from the Lord."* This is the last selection of leaders by lot recorded in the New Testament. Following the promised spiritual outpouring, choosing leaders will become the Holy Spirit's task.

Personalize this lesson.

☑ In the first chapter of Acts, we see Peter and Judas, two disciples who sinned against God through their denial and betrayal. Both suffer consequences for their sins, but their lives go in entirely different directions because of their responses to God's offer of forgiveness.

Judas's final act is one of despair and defeat. Judas's anguish wasn't the godly grief that leads to repentance and salvation; it was worldly sorrow that produces death.

Peter didn't despair either of himself or of God. In John 21:15-19, we're told of his meeting with the risen Savior, where it's evident he received His forgiveness. Jesus not only forgives but also restores the truly repentant. In Acts 2, we'll see the great extent to which Peter is restored—he will become the spokesman for the believers on the day of Pentecost and will preach the first sermon of the newly established church.

Fellowship with God and being useful to Him does not depend on our never making mistakes, but on our constantly being renewed by receiving His forgiveness. Ask God to show you if there is any sin in your life—past or present—for which you have not received His forgiveness. If there is, confess it and ask Him to restore you. Thank Him that because of Jesus, you can put your sins behind you and play a significant role in the kingdom of God.

The Festival With a Surprise
Acts 2:1-21

Memorize God's Word: Acts 2:17.

❖ Acts 2:1-4—The Day of Pentecost Arrives

1. What promise that Jesus made to His followers is now fulfilled (Matthew 3:11; Acts 1:5-8)?

    _____

    _____

2. How does one receive or become sealed in the Holy Spirit (Galatians 3:2; Ephesians 1:13-14)?

    _____

    _____

❖ Selected Verses—The Holy Spirit

3. According to 2 Corinthians 3:18, what does the Holy Spirit do in our lives?

    _____

    _____

4. From Galatians 5:22-23, list the character qualities that the Holy Spirit can produce in our lives.

    _____

    _____

    _____

5. What changes have you seen the Holy Spirit make in your life?

    _____

    _____

    _____

    _____

6. From the following verses, describe some other ministries of the
    Holy Spirit.

    a. John 16:7-11 _____

        _____

        _____

    b. John 16:13-15 _____

        _____

        _____

    c. Romans 8:26-27_____

        _____

        _____

7. What command about the Holy Spirit is given in Ephesians 5:18?

    _____

    _____

8. What are some results of being filled with the Holy Spirit?

    a. Acts 4:31 _____

        _____

        _____

    b. Acts 13:8-10 _____

        _____

        _____

    c. Acts 13:52 _____

        _____

        _____

❖ Acts 2:5-21—Peter Responds to The Crowds

9. What words does Luke use to describe the crowd's reaction to the outpouring of the Spirit (6-7, 12)?

_____

_____

_____

10. In Peter's response, what will God's people do when He pours out His Spirit (17-18)?

_____

_____

11. Using a dictionary, record several variations of the meaning of *prophesy*.

_____

_____

_____

12. When are *"the last days"* (2:17)? (See also Hebrews 1:1-2; 1 Peter 1:18-20.)

_____

_____

_____

13. What do you think Peter means by the *"day of the Lord"* (2:20)? (See also 2 Peter 3:10-13.)

_____

_____

14. According to verses 20-21, who will be saved?

_____

_____

_____

Apply what you have learned. Review the different ways in which the Spirit works in a believer. In which of these areas would you most like to experience more of the Spirit's impact in your life? Reflect on how you might better allow the Spirit to work in this area. Then write out a prayer, asking the Holy Spirit to fill you, empower you, and change you.

The Festival With a Surprise
Acts 2:1-21

The gift of the Holy Spirit given on the day of Israel's Feast of Pentecost is one of the central events of salvation history. This gift marks the beginning of the church and enables the work Jesus began in His earthly ministry to continue through His followers.

Prelude to Pentecost

In the previous chapter, Jesus instructed His disciples: *"Wait for the promise of the Father ... you will be baptized with the Holy Spirit"* (1:4-5). The first phrase of chapter 2—*"When the day of Pentecost arrived"*—sets the scene of the event for which the small group of believers has been waiting.

The Old Testament Pentecost festival (also called the Feast of Weeks, the Feast of Harvest, and the Day of Firstfruits) was one of three annual occasions that every faithful Jew living within 20 miles of Jerusalem came to the Holy City to observe. (The other two were the Feast of Tabernacles and Passover.) In Jesus' day, Jerusalem had a population of 50,000. During the high holy days, that number increased to as many as half a million. Pentecost was held later in the spring than Passover, when sea travel was less treacherous. Therefore, Jews living on the rim of the Mediterranean could come together to celebrate as well.

Israel's barley harvest began about the time of Passover, the annual feast commemorating the nation's exodus from Egypt. Fifty days later, the first harvest of wheat was gathered and the prime fruit or grain was brought to the festival of Pentecost as a sacrifice. On the day of Pentecost referred to in Acts, the small group of believers can be seen as the "firstfruits" of a bountiful harvest of converts to come. Judaism's celebration of Pentecost in remembrance of the giving of the old covenant also parallels the Christian celebration of Pentecost, which remembers the giving of the new covenant and the gift of the Holy Spirit. The first Christian Pentecost, a time of rejoicing, is consistent with the mood of the Jewish festival.

A Sound Like a Mighty Rushing Wind

Although the disciples are expecting something special to happen, nothing could have prepared them for what was about to take place at Pentecost. Morning prayer time at the temple is interrupted by a thunderous sound *"like a mighty rushing wind"* (2:2). The unusual sound undoubtedly draws people into the streets to investigate, some of whom will likely be among the 3,000 souls added to the church that day. Then, *"tongues as of fire"* appear on the 120 believers. This combination of sights and sounds parallels Psalm 104:4: *"He makes His messengers winds, His ministers a flaming fire."*

Think about the glorious gift that came to us at Pentecost. For the first time in history, the Holy Spirit came to live in believers. The Old Testament records instances of the Holy Spirit coming upon a person for a specific purpose (Judges 14:6; 1 Samuel 10:10), but these were only temporary visits.

Paul speaks of the Holy Spirit as being a Person: *"And do not grieve the Holy Spirit of God, by whom you were sealed for the day of redemption"* (Ephesians 4:30). The word grieve indicates that we not only respond to the Holy Spirit, but He responds to us; we have a personal relationship with Him. Scripture assures that believers have been sealed with the Holy Spirit—that is, permanently marked as belonging to God. Because of these two important truths—that the Holy Spirit lives in us, and that we forever be-long to Him—we can be confident that God is always with us.

Believers Speak in Other Tongues

The giving of the Holy Spirit at Pentecost is a giant step forward in God's plan to gather a people who will acknowledge Him as Lord. Luke tells us the believers gathered that day *"were all filled with the Holy Spirit and began to speak in other tongues"* (Acts 2:4). Pentecost is a Tower of Babel experience in reverse. At Pentecost, rather than scattering the people and giving them different tongues to prevent a united rebellion of mankind (Genesis 11:1-9), God uses diverse languages to unify the people, so they can hear the wonders of God expressed in their own regional speech, the languages close to their hearts.

The believers' miraculous speech on Pentecost morning becomes a powerful sign that the God of all nations is fulfilling what the prophets foretold: *"The time is coming to gather all nations and tongues. And they shall come and shall see My glory, and I will set a sign among them"* (Isaiah 66:18-19).

The members of the crowd are *"amazed and perplexed"* (Acts 2:12) because they hear men from Galilee witnessing to God's mighty works in at least 12 different languages from places as far away as Mesopotamia and Cyrene in Libya. Unfortunately, not all those gathered in the crowd marvel at the sights and sounds before them. Some mock the believers, remarking that they are drunk with wine.

Peter Explains Pentecost

Peter responds to the amazed crowd's question: *"What does this mean?"* (2:12). He counters the mockers. This is not drunkenness; rather, it is the work of God's Spirit, prophesied by Joel: *"In the last days … God declares, 'I will pour out My Spirit on all flesh'"* (2:17). Peter knew the authority Scripture had among the God-fearing Jews gathered that day. Old Testament believers longed for a time when God would send His Spirit on all people, not just a few select leaders.

Personalize this lesson.

The Holy Spirit dwells in all believers. His presence in our lives is constant and unconditional. But we may resist the Spirit (Acts 7:51) and may even *"quench"* the Spirit's fire (1 Thessalonians 5:19). Based on your experience and your knowledge of Scripture, what are some ways in which believers block what the Spirit wants to do in their lives? Prayerfully ask God if you have any unconfessed sins, fears, attitudes, or anything else that is interfering with the Spirit's work in you. If you sense a need for change, tell Him about it and ask Him to help you better cooperate with His good plan for you.

The Church Begins to Grow
Acts 2:22-47

Memorize God's Word: Acts 2:38.

❖ Acts 2:22-23—Peter Describes Christ's Uniqueness

1. What do you think helps Peter preach his sermon with authority?

   _____

   _____

2. What are some of the *"mighty works and wonders and signs that God did"* (22:22) through Jesus?

   _____

   _____

   _____

3. Acts 2:23 states that Jesus was crucified *"according to the definite plan and foreknowledge of God."* Isaiah 53 is a prophecy and explanation of Jesus' death on the cross. According to Isaiah 53:10-12, what did Jesus accomplish through His death?

   _____

   _____

4. How does Jesus' death on the cross affect you personally?

   _____

   _____

   _____

❖ Acts 2:24-28—Peter Relates the Resurrection to Old Testament Prophecy

5. Peter says, *"it was not possible for Him to be held by* [death]*"* (2:24). What does he mean?

    _____

    _____

6. How does the truth of John 11:25-26 apply to your life?

    _____

    _____

    _____

7. In Acts 2:26-28, how does David predict the resurrection of the Messiah and relate it to his own life?

    _____

    _____

    _____

❖ Acts 2:29-36—Peter Declares That the Resurrection Verifies Jesus' Deity

8. How does David's death David differ from Jesus' death?

    _____

    _____

    _____

9. What do the following verses state about the significance of the Resurrection?

    a. Acts 17:31 _____

       _____

    b. Romans 5:10 _____

       _____

    c. Romans 6:9-11 _____

       _____

d. Philippians 3:20-21 _____

_____

10. Which of these verses is most meaningful to you? Why?

_____

_____

❖ Acts 2:37-41—Peter Urges His Fellow Jews to Repent

11. Acts 2:37 says the men of Israel were *"cut to the heart"* with Peter's message. Describe what you think this means.

_____

_____

12. What does Peter tell them to do with their guilt?

_____

_____

13. Read Acts 26:20 and Matthew 3:8. From these verses, how do you define the word *repent*? (For additional help, use a dictionary.)

_____

_____

14. Peter gives a sermon on the resurrected Christ in Jerusalem, where His resurrection occurred. Apparently, nobody in the crowd challenges or denies his statements about Christ's resurrection. What do you think is significant about this?

_____

_____

15. What word does Peter use to describe the generation to whom he is speaking? How do you define that word?

_____

_____

16. What significance does the risen Christ have for our generation?

_____

_____

❖ Acts 2:42-47—The Holy Spirit Is Displayed in the Lives of New Believers

17. Try to list at least seven different *attitudes* in the group of new believers.

_____

_____

18. What various actions characterize their lives?

_____

_____

19. How do their attitudes and actions relate to Jesus' statement in Luke 6:44-45?

_____

_____

Apply what you have learned. The first believers did more than give mental assent to the message of the Resurrection, they wrapped their lives around it. People noticed, and they, too, believed. Review the attitudes and actions you listed in questions 17 and 18. Choose one that you think God might want to be a more important part of your life. What is one step you can take this week to devote yourself to this demonstration of your faith?

The Church Begins to Grow
Acts 2:22-47

After the Holy Spirit comes upon believers at Pentecost, Peter addresses the thousands of awestruck witnesses. He speaks of God's miraculous work through Jesus, telling the crowd how they can invite Him into their lives.

The First Christian Sermon

After Peter defends his fellow believers' seemingly unusual behavior, he launches into the first sermon recorded after Jesus' death and resurrection. Peter's speech in Acts 2:22-36 focuses on Jesus rather than on the people's sin. The Holy Spirit allows Peter to recognize that people do not have a clear picture of sin until they have seen the Sinless One.

A Man Accredited by God

Most of those in Peter's audience had seen or heard of Jesus, and knew of His healings and miracles. Generally, people reacted to Him in one of three ways: (1) they believed in Him and became His followers; (2) they accepted the Pharisees' accusation that He did miracles by the power of Satan; or (3) they put off making any decision about Him at all—in itself a decision, a kind of denial of Him. Peter insists that Jesus had to have been empowered by God, not Satan, to perform the miracles, signs, and wonders that He did (Acts 2:22).

According to God's Plan and Foreknowledge

Peter continues, *"This Jesus* [was] *delivered up according to the definite plan and foreknowledge of God"* (2:23). Peter's point here is that while God hates evil, in His graciousness and mercy He uses even the wicked and sinful things people do—like crucifying a sinless man—to work out His purposes.

People Are Accountable for Their Sins

Although God is sovereign and uses even people's evil deeds for His purposes, He holds us responsible for our actions: Jesus was *"crucified and killed by the hands of lawless men"* (Acts 2:23). Perhaps some of the men Peter addresses were sorry to see Jesus fall into His enemies' hands, but they took no action. Others may have been in the crowd that shouted, *"Let Him be crucified!"* (Matthew 27:22-23). Peter confronts all of his listeners with their responsibility for Jesus' death.

Think about the part we played in Jesus' Crucifixion. We can easily rationalize our personal sins away until we are face-to-face with Jesus. Only when we begin to "see" the Sinless One do we have any real concept of our own sin. Jesus fulfilled the divine plan by dying on the Cross. He died not because some evil men in the first century demanded it, but because all people who have lived or will live require it due to their sin. We can find encouragement knowing His death made forgiveness available to all!

The Resurrection—A New Hope

To Old Testament believers, the existence of an afterlife was a vague hope. But Peter states that what was only a hope in Old Testament times is made a reality through Christ's resurrection. Peter quotes David's prophecy of this resurrection: *"You will not abandon my soul to Hades, or let your Holy One see corruption"* (Acts 2:27). Jesus was raised to heaven and shares in God's action, even as He did before the Incarnation. Jesus also received the fullness of the Spirit from the Father.

Peter concludes by stating that Jesus and God are one: *"God has made Him both Lord* [supreme authority] *and Christ* [Greek form of the Hebrew Messiah], *this Jesus whom you crucified"* (2:36).

Think about the Resurrection as the central event in history. The Resurrection validates Jesus, God's only Son, as Savior and Lord. Because of it—and only because of it—we have hope: *"If Christ has not*

been raised, your faith is futile and you are still in your sins"
(1 Corinthians 15:17). The Resurrection gives meaning to
life and frees us from bondage to sin and death. We are not
yet perfect, but we are on the way. The Spirit of Christ, the
same power that raised Jesus from the dead (Romans 8:11),
is working within us to make us as righteous as God has
declared us to be (2 Corinthians 3:18). We are commanded,
therefore, to rely on the Lord's work in our lives and to give
ourselves wholeheartedly in His service.

The Response of Faith

In response to Peter's sermon, many of those gathered are *"cut to the
heart,"* remorseful for having rejected Christ. They ask, *"What shall we
do?"* (Acts 2:37). Peter responds, *"Repent and be baptized every one of
you, in the name of Jesus Christ for the forgiveness of your sins, and you will
receive the gift of the Holy Spirit"* (Acts 2:38). Following Peter's call, 3,000
people are baptized and added to the church that day.

Evidence of a Spirit-Filled Church

The group of new believers, empowered by the Holy Spirit, form a
"witnessing" church with an evangelistic drive. Their activities center on
apostolic teaching, sharing, the breaking of bread, and prayer. Acts 2:42-
47 summarizes their practices:

❖ Devoted to the apostles' teaching—The need for instruction is
   a primary concern of the early church. The Lord commanded
   the disciples to teach future believers *"to observe all that I have
   commanded you"* (Matthew 28:19-20).

❖ Fellowship—Fellowship is characterized by a genuine concern for
   others and a willingness to share one's goods with those less fortunate.
   What believers have in common—Christ—is more important than
   anything that might divide them. From the beginning, believers
   "broke bread," or ate together, in one another's homes.

❖ Worship and prayer—Prayer, an integral part of worship in the early
   church, involves praising and thanking God, and praying for one's self
   and others. The early believers had both formal times of prayer in the
   synagogues and informal prayer meetings in homes.

Personalize this lesson.

✓ The believers loved Jesus and each other so much that they shared all they had with one another. While such communal sharing did not exist everywhere, great willingness in all the churches to help one another in practical ways was and continues to be the mark of Christians (1 John 3:17-18).

Freely giving away our possessions requires selflessness, trust in God's provision, and the conviction that everything we have is a gift from God. Spend some time praying about your attitude toward your money and possessions. Are you able to hold them with an open hand, willing to do with them whatever God asks? Ask God to grow you into, or help you continue to be, a person with a *"generous heart"* (Acts 2:46).

Power in Word and in Deed
Acts 3

❖ Acts 3:1-10—Peter and John Heal a Lame Beggar

1. Why are Peter and John going to the temple?

   _____

   _____

2. How often does this beggar go to the temple gate, and who would have seen him?

   _____

   _____

   _____

3. Because Jesus often went to the temple, He must have seen the beggar many times. Why do you think Jesus did not heal the man, and what can you learn from this? Give several different thoughts.

   _____

   _____

   _____

   _____

   _____

4. What power does Peter use to heal the lame man?

   _____

   _____

❖ Acts 3:1-10—Reaction to and Significance of the Healing

5. How does the lame man's react to the healing?

    _____

    _____

6. How does the crowd react?

    _____

    _____

7. What do you learn from this incident that you can apply to your life?

    _____

    _____

    _____

    _____

❖ Acts 3:11-16—Peter Explains How the Lame Man Was Healed

8. Whom does Peter credit with this healing?

    _____

    _____

9. In verse 13, Peter states that God *"glorified His servant Jesus."* The dictionary defines *glorify* as *exalting or giving honor to.* According to the following verses, how does God reveal the glory of His servant Jesus?

    a. John 1:14 _____

        _____

    b. Hebrews 1:3_____

        _____

    c. Hebrews 2:9_____

        _____

10. According to the following verses, what does the title *"Author of life"* (3:15) mean?

    a. John 1:3-4 _____

    _____

    b. John 5:21, 24 _____

    _____

11. What do you think *"faith in His name"* (Acts 3:16) means?

    _____

    _____

❖ Acts 3:17-21—Peter Urges His Fellow Jews to Repent

12. As you reflect on Lesson 4, what does the word *repent* mean?

    _____

    _____

13. What are two immediate results of repentance?

    _____

    _____

    _____

14. What other reason does Peter give to repent? (See also 2 Peter 3:9-12.)

    _____

    _____

15. How would you explain the claim that turning to God in repentance will wipe out our sins? (See also 2 Corinthians 5:21; Hebrews 9:26; 1 John 3:5.)

    _____

    _____

    _____

    _____

❖ Acts 3:19-26—The Consequences of Receiving or Rejecting the Message

16. From these verses, list some reasons God sent Jesus to earth.

_____

_____

17. What is the consequence for those who reject Christ and His message?

_____

_____

18. What does Jesus say will happen to those who reject His message?

   a.   Matthew 10:33 _____

   _____

   b.   Mark 16:16_____

   _____

   c.   John 8:24, 12:48_____

   _____

Apply what you have learned. The consequences of rejecting Jesus are sobering. Make a list of five to ten people you know who have not received Jesus. For the remainder of the time you are doing this study, pray daily that each one will become a believer.

Power in Word and in Deed
Acts 3

In Acts 2, Peter emerges as a prominent leader in the early church as he addresses a confused and awestruck crowd at Pentecost. In Acts 3, he takes advantage of another opportunity to share God's Word with the people of Israel.

A Successful Venture

At 3 p.m., Peter and John make their way to the temple for prayer. At about the same time, a beggar, lame from birth, is carried to the gate called "Beautiful" where he sits each day to beg. He asks Peter and John for money. Probably to the beggar's puzzlement and disappointment, Peter replies, *"I have no silver and gold, but what I do have I give to you. In the name of Jesus Christ of Nazareth, rise up and walk!"* (Acts 3:6). Peter takes the man by the hand to raise him up. Instantly, the beggar's feet and ankles become strong; he leaps, walks, and goes with the disciples into the temple, praising God.

Others in the town recognize the man and are amazed at his transformation. Many who witness this miracle must have been reminded of Jesus' healing of the man who had been crippled for 38 years. That man's healing at Bethesda's porches increased the Jews' opposition toward Jesus because He told the healed man to carry his bed; the rulers criticized both the man and Jesus for working on a Sabbath day—a day of rest. In a similar way, the healing of the beggar marks the beginning of trouble for Peter and for Jesus' followers, as we will see in later chapters.

Think about the healing of the lame beggar as a new demonstration of God's amazing goodness. At the gate Beautiful, a request for a very small favor—a few coins—is answered by the large, unexpected gift of healing. Peter, inspired by the Holy Spirit, did not answer the man's spoken request, but the deep need of his heart—to be whole.

Many of our prayers are beggars' prayers. Like the beggar, we ask for a few miserable coins, never dreaming of asking for wholeness. Sometimes our prayers seem unanswered because we are looking for a small answer to a small prayer. We fail to see God's response because it is not what we asked for and expected.

Pray to God honestly about your heart's desires. You will receive a blessing from Him—perhaps one far beyond what you asked for.

What's in a Name?

The news of the healed beggar spreads, and a mob soon gathers. Peter seizes the opportunity to preach another sermon, urging the assembled group to believe in their Messiah. Peter asks the crowd, *"Why do you wonder at this, … as though by our own power or piety we have made him walk? The God of Abraham, the God of Isaac, and the God of Jacob, the God of our fathers, glorified His servant Jesus"* (Acts 3:12-13). He speaks of Abraham, Isaac, and Jacob to connect the Jewish crowd with their past, their heritage that records centuries of God's miracles. He emphasizes that this miracle of healing, like the ones recorded in the Old Testament, can only be God's doing. Peter and John simply acted as ambassadors of God's kingdom, agents of the Lord Jesus Christ.

Peter also says God healed the beggar to glorify *"His servant"* (3:13). Peter's word choice refers to the Suffering Servant prophesied by Isaiah. The people listening probably wondered, "Who is this servant of God?" Before they can ask, Peter tells them that Jesus fulfills every Messianic hope and prediction.

Peter's boldness in the face of increasing hostility from his audience borders on the miraculous. He chides them for delivering Jesus up to be crucified. He continues to fault them for not being able to discern that Jesus was the *"Holy and Righteous One"* (Acts 3:14). The phrase *"Holy One of Israel"* occurs three times in Psalms and 26 times in Isaiah, each time with a prophetic intent. The phrase would therefore have been familiar to Peter's audience. How devastating to these men to hear that title used to refer to Jesus, whose life they had bartered away for the life of the murderer Barabbas.

Peter directly accuses the Jews of murder, the victim being *"the Author of life"* (3:15). Jesus is God the Son. God created the world and all life through Him; God sustains all life through Him. The supreme blasphemy, the ultimate irony, is for created beings who have received life through Christ to take His physical life from the Creator.

Despite the Jews' act of ignorance, God raised Jesus from the dead and made the disciples witnesses of His resurrection. Peter explains that Jesus' name and the faith that comes through Him is what healed the lame man. The risen Christ and the beggar's faith in Him is what make him whole.

Peter Pleads With the Men of Israel

A note of tenderness and mercy emerges in verse 17. As a member of the same nation, of the same blood, and a fellow heir of the heritage of Abraham, Isaac, and Jacob, Peter pleads with his *"brothers."* He does not excuse them; their guilt for crucifying their Savior cannot be denied. But God, in His mercy, is ready to answer Jesus' prayer on the Cross: *"Father, forgive them, for they know not what they do"* (Luke 23:34). If they are sorry for their sins, ask God for forgiveness, and turn their lives over to Him, their sins will be wiped out.

Peter tells the crowd that Christ must remain in heaven until God sends Him to restore everything, as He promised long ago through Moses and the prophets. Peter reminds his listeners that *they* are the heirs of the prophets and the sons of the covenant—that God desires to bless them especially. Peter supports his statement by saying God raised up Jesus and sent Him to Israel first. Peter's appeal to his listeners, using Old Testament prophecy known to them, should have been very persuasive. He hopes that in the light of the Crucifixion and Resurrection, the Old Testament will have new meaning.

Personalize this lesson.

In Acts 3:19-20, Peter implores the Jews, *"Repent therefore, and turn again, that your sins may be blotted out, that times of refreshing may come from the presence of the Lord."* What a beautiful invitation! Can you think of a time when you experienced "times of refreshing" after turning from sin? Ask God to show you if there is anything in your life right now that is interfering with your ability to experience God's presence, and for which you need to repent. Thank Him for His wonderful, ongoing offer of forgiveness and restored fellowship.

The Church Under Attack
Acts 4

❖ Acts 4:1-4—Peter and John Imprisoned

1. What were some of the people's reactions to the message of the Resurrection?

    _____

    _____

    _____

2. What reactions do people have to the Resurrection today?

    _____

    _____

    _____

3. What do the priests, temple guards, and Sadducees do with Peter and John?

    _____

    _____

❖ Acts 4:5-12—Peter Preaches to the Sanhedrin

4. How does Peter explain the healing of the lame man to the Sanhedrin?

    _____

    _____

    _____

5. Consider how Peter speaks to crowds of common people and aristocratic leaders with equal authority. Where does Peter get this authority?

    _____

    _____

6. Have you experienced God giving you power to speak about Him to others? If so, give an example of one such instance.

    _____

    _____

    _____

    _____

7. Jesus is described as *"the stone ... which has become the cornerstone"* (4:11). Use a dictionary to define *cornerstone*.

    _____

    _____

8. How does the definition apply to Christ? (See also Psalm 118:22-23 and Isaiah 28:16.)

    _____

    _____

    _____

9. Rewrite verse 12 in your own words, as though you were explaining it to a person who asks you, "How does the Bible say a person can be saved?"

    _____

    _____

    _____

10. What words would you use to describe Peter's statement here?

    _____

    _____

    _____

❖ Acts 4:13-22—The Jewish Council Marvels at Peter and John

11. The religious leaders recognize that the apostles *"had been with Jesus"* (4:13). What can we do today in order to "be with Jesus"?

_____

_____

12. How might people be able to tell you have been with Him?

_____

_____

❖ Acts 4:23-31—Peter and John Report to Their Companions

13. How do Peter and John's friends respond when they hear the Council meeting report?

_____

_____

14. For what do they pray?

_____

15. How does God answer their prayer?

_____

_____

❖ Acts 4:32-36—Faith and Action

16. What attitudes and behaviors do the new believers adopt?

_____

_____

17. What do the new believers and the apostles receive from God at this time?

_____

_____

18. Verse 32 describes the complete harmony among the believers. How do you think Christians can experience this kind of harmony today?

_____

_____

19. Verse 34 shows that God so fills the believers that they are released from their love of material possessions. How can we experience this same freedom?

_____

_____

20. Verse 36 introduces Barnabas, an important man in the development of the early Christian movement. List at least three characteristics of his personality.

_____

_____

_____

_____

Apply what you have learned. In Acts 4, Peter, John, and their friends display boldness in their new life in Christ. In which area of your life would you like to see this kind of boldness? Ask the Holy Spirit to give you strength and courage to break out of your comfort zone this week.

The Church Under Attack
Acts 4

The first three chapters of Acts record one triumph after another: Christ's ascension and resurrection, the gift of the Holy Spirit, the apostles' preaching and healing ministry, and the growing reputation of the church. But just as Christ endured great suffering while on earth, so, too, does the church. In Acts 4, we see how Satan works through the established religious authorities to try to hamper the Holy Spirit's work in the infant church.

Peter and John Before the Council

In response to the lame man's healing, crowds gather in the temple courts. As Peter and John preach the Resurrection, the Sadducees, priests, captain of the temple guard, and other enemies of Jesus become greatly disturbed.

The political situation in Jerusalem at the time reveals why the church was being challenged. The two main religious parties, the Pharisees and Sadducees, shared few of the same beliefs, yet united in opposing Jesus. The Sadducees, a group that included the priests, were landowners who were considered to be Israel's nobility. They held traditional socioeconomic views but liberal religious beliefs. Unlike the Pharisees, they did not believe in a bodily resurrection or in angels or demons. They thought of Christians as radicals, guilty of disturbing their thinking and way of life.

Insistence on keeping the Law characterized the Pharisees. The Pharisees maintained their authority and resisted Greek and Roman influence on Judaism. And like the Sadducees, their desire to protect and preserve the existing state of affairs put them in conflict with Jesus.

The Jewish authorities seize Peter and his young companion, John. The Sadducees are angered because Jesus' followers not only confront the crowds with Jesus' resurrection, they also teach resurrection as an event to be anticipated by everyone. About 5,000 people convert out of a total population of 25,000 to 30,000. No wonder Annas, the high priest, and Caiaphas, Annas's son-in-law, feel threatened. The authorities jail Peter and John until morning when they will stand trial.

Think about why Jesus' death and resurrection always have been and will continue to be under attack despite the evidence that supports these events. One reason for this attack involves the Cross, God's final judgment on sin. Admitting personal sinfulness strikes at the heart of human pride, causing many people to refuse to heed the Holy Spirit. Only the Holy Spirit enables us to say, "Christ's death on the cross was for *my* sins."

In addition, the resurrected Christ demands total commitment from His followers. Obedience is an unpopular concept among those whose universe revolves around themselves, who want a God they can control, who want to give orders rather than receive them. Today, many people continue to fight the reality of Christ's death, resurrection, and ascension for the same reasons the Pharisees and Sadducees did.

A Great Preaching Opportunity

Peter seized every opportunity to preach the good news about Jesus. Now appearing before the Sanhedrin, the Jewish supreme court, Peter has a chance to speak to the same people who tried his Master. The Sanhedrin was composed of high priests, tribal elders of the Jewish families, and scribes—Pharisees and Sadducees. In New Testament times, the scribes were teachers of the Law and generally aligned with the Pharisee party, while members of the priestly families identified themselves as Sadducees.

Avoiding the divisive issue of the Resurrection, members of the Sanhedrin ask Peter *"by what power or by what name"* (4:7) he had healed the lame man. The temple authorities apparently suspect use of "black magic" in the name of Satan. Peter, filled with the Holy Spirit, explains that the crippled man was healed by the name of Jesus of Nazareth. He tells them that Jesus is *"the stone that was rejected by you, the builders"* (4:11), the only One who has the power to heal and to save: *"There is salvation in no one else, for there is no other name under heaven given among men by which we must be saved"* (4:12).

Think about Peter's reference to Jesus as the Stone. Jesus used the same symbolism of the rejected stone in referring to Himself in a parable recorded in all three Synoptic Gospels (Matthew 21:33-42; Mark 12:1-11; Luke 20:9-19). The "stone" metaphor illustrates biblical truth: A stone can either crush or become a precious foundation. Similarly, the gospel is both bad and good news: The bad news warns of His justice if His love is refused; the good news is God's mercy, love, and grace. God has given us His best in His Son, but God's judgment remains for those who reject Him.

Men Who Couldn't Be Silenced

The Sanhedrin is astonished by Peter's bold responses. They dismiss the lame man and the disciples so they can discuss the situation privately. Realizing they do not have a case, the Sanhedrin asks the disciples to return, issues them a stern warning, and commands them not to speak in Jesus' name again. The disciples refuse, explaining that God has commanded them to witness. Because Peter and his company are popular with the multitude, the Sanhedrin decides not to risk punishing them further. After threatening Peter and John again, they let them go.

Peter and John hurry to tell their friends what happened. Everyone joins in praying from Psalm 2. After praising God for who He is, what He has said, and what He has done, they ask for more boldness, power, and persuasiveness in sharing Jesus with others. The Holy Spirit fills the believers, and the meeting place shakes. The earthquake serves as a sign of God's willingness to be with them in the anticipated difficulties ahead.

Joseph, Called Barnabas

Next, we see the Holy Spirit's working to unite the early Christians. Believers freely share all their material possessions and are *"of one heart and soul."* The Spirit prompts one man, Joseph, whom the apostles call *"Barnabas,"* to sell a piece of his property and lay the proceeds at the disciples' feet. As we learn later in Acts, Barnabas is the first Christian missionary.

Personalize this lesson.

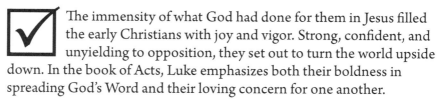 The immensity of what God had done for them in Jesus filled the early Christians with joy and vigor. Strong, confident, and unyielding to opposition, they set out to turn the world upside down. In the book of Acts, Luke emphasizes both their boldness in spreading God's Word and their loving concern for one another.

Which of these characteristics of the early church—boldness in proclaiming Christ or giving sacrificially to help needy Christians—comes most easily to you? Which is more difficult? Thank God for the ways in which He has worked through you in either of these areas. Then ask His Spirit to enable you to better display His power in your weaker area.

Stormy Days for the Church
Acts 5

❖ **Acts 5:1-11—God Punishes Ananias and Sapphira**

1. How do Ananias and Sapphira sin, and whom do they sin against?

   _____

   _____

2. In Scripture, people's names often denote their character. Describe Satan's character from his names given in the following verses:

   a. Matthew 13:19 _____

   _____

   b. Revelation 12:9 _____

   _____

3. What do you think Satan is trying to accomplish by successfully tempting Ananias and Sapphira to lie? What can you learn from this?

   _____

   _____

4. What consequence(s) of lying to the Holy Spirit do Ananias and Sapphira experience?

   _____

   _____

5. Which attributes of God do you see in this punishment?

_____

_____

❖ Acts 5:12-16—God Surrounds the Apostles' Ministry With Signs and Wonders

6. What kinds of miracles do the apostles perform here, and what are the results?

_____

_____

_____

7. According to Matthew 13:57-58, what is one reason God sometimes chooses not to perform miracles?

_____

_____

8. Read Matthew 17:19-20, and explain what is necessary for a person to experience God's miraculous power today.

_____

_____

_____

❖ Acts 5:17-32—Imprisoned by the Jewish Council, Freed by an Angel

9. Why do you think the Jewish religious leaders are jealous of the apostles?

_____

_____

10. What attitudes do the leaders display toward the apostles in this passage?

_____

_____

11. In Acts 5:19-20, *"an angel of the Lord opened the prison doors and brought* [the apostles] *out."* What other ministries do angels perform?

    a. Psalm 91:11 _____

    _____

    b. Luke 2:9-13 _____

    _____

    _____

    c. Hebrews 1:14 _____

    _____

12. What instructions does the angel give to the apostles, and how do they respond (5:20-21)?

    _____

    _____

    _____

13. Why does Peter say they disobeyed the Jewish leaders' command not to teach about Jesus?

    _____

    _____

❖ Acts 5:33-39—Gamaliel Intervenes

14. How does the opposition to the apostles' witnessing about Jesus progress according to Acts 4–5?

    _____

    _____

    _____

    _____

15. Who is Gamaliel, and what kind of man is he?

    _____

    _____

16. What logic does Gamaliel use to stop the Jewish leaders from putting the apostles to death?

_____

_____

❖ Acts 5:40-42—The Council Releases the Apostles

17. Read Matthew 5:11-12. How did the apostles' reaction to opposition display the attitude Jesus taught?

_____

_____

18. What do you think enables the apostles to respond in this way?

_____

_____

19. Review each of the headings in this lesson. To you, which situation is the most meaningful demonstration of God's miraculous intervention, and why?

Acts 5:1-11— God Punishes Ananias and Sapphira

Acts 5:12-16—God Surrounds the Apostles' Ministry With Signs and Wonders

Acts 5:17-32—Imprisoned by the Jewish Council, Freed by an Angel

Acts 5:33-39—Gamaliel Intervenes

Acts 5:40-42—The Council Releases the Apostles

Apply what you have learned. This passage ends with, _"And every day … they did not cease teaching and preaching that the Christ is Jesus."_ What are some ways that you could teach or preach about Jesus this week? Choose one and do it.

Stormy Days for the Church
Acts 5

In chapter 5, Luke completes his account of the church's witness to the Jewish community in Jerusalem before the gospel goes out to the ends of the earth. More periods of rejoicing contrast with the young church's trials.

Deception and Judgment

Ananias sells some property so that he, like Barnabas, can give a gift to the church. However, while Barnabas gave openly and freely with no strings attached, Ananias, with the knowledge and consent of his wife, Sapphira, presents the money to the apostles but secretly keeps back a portion of it. Seeing through the lie, Peter asks Ananias, *"Why has Satan filled your heart to lie to the Holy Spirit? ... You have not lied to men but to God"* (5:3-4). Upon hearing this, Ananias falls down and dies. Three hours later, Sapphira appears on the scene. When Peter notifies her of her husband's death and confronts her with their sin, she lies also, and dies in the same manner. Ananias's pallbearers are just returning from burying his body when Sapphira is struck down, and they bury her at his side. The tragic consequences of this couple's deceit provide a sobering lesson for the early church.

Ananias and Sapphira's sin is not about withholding some of the money from the church, but in lying about the matter. They want the best of both worlds: credit for sacrificial giving without having to trust God to provide for their future.

Why was God's judgment on Ananias so severe? One answer may be that in those first days of the church, its members' integrity was crucial. Had God allowed Ananias and Sapphira to go unpunished, the example they set might have spread. Whatever His reason, God is sovereign. This severe lesson is hard for the church to learn, but one God sees as important to teach. As a result, the church develops a healthy respect for God.

> ☘ **Think about** how God's quick judgment on Ananias and Sapphira reminds us of the seriousness of all sin. Ananias and Sapphira's sin was obvious, but less conspicuous sins can be just as damaging to the church and to us individually. Whatever is not compatible with Christian character is a hindrance to the spread of the gospel.

Fear in Spite of Signs and Wonders

The apostles continue to perform miracles among the people. Some of those witnessing the signs and wonders are frightened by the Sanhedrin and the temple guard, but quietly continue to admire the apostles. Multitudes become believers. Crowds gather on the streets, many coming from neighboring towns. They bring their sick and those afflicted with evil spirits, and Luke says, *"they were all healed"* (5:16). Few other recorded instances exist of everyone being healed; God is validating the message and the messengers.

> ☘ **Think about** Jesus' miracles as evidence of His Messiahship—a sign of God's presence and approval. In the same way, the signs and wonders done by the apostles were an indication God was acting in the members of His infant church. The Old Testament recounts many miraculous signs of God's intervention for His people. Nevertheless, the Israelites' history is one of recurring disobedience. The signs and wonders were not enough to keep them faithful to God.

Iron Bars Do Not a Prison Make

Filled with jealousy, the high priest and his fellow Sadducees imprison the apostles for the second time. Because God still has important work for them to do, an angel of the Lord opens the door of the jail to free them. The angel instructs the apostles to stand in the temple courts and speak to the people *"all the words of this Life"* (Acts 5:20). That message includes what God offers everyone in Jesus: forgiveness of sin, salvation, and eternal life.

When members of the temple guard are sent to the prison to bring the apostles to trial, they find no one inside. Shortly thereafter, someone reports the apostles are *"standing in the temple and teaching the people"* (5:25). Upon hearing this, the captain and his officers escort the apostles (without force for fear of the crowd's reaction) to appear before the Sanhedrin and high priest, Caiaphas, for questioning. Caiaphas reads the citation to the apostles, and reminds them of the Sanhedrin's earlier warning to stop teaching about Jesus. *"'We strictly charged you not to teach in this name, yet here you have filled Jerusalem with your teaching, and you intend to bring this man's blood upon us'"* (5:28). The apostles answer that their consciences require them to obey God rather than men, and they must teach of the resurrected Christ *"whom you killed by hanging Him on a tree"* (5:30).

Rejoicing in Suffering

Infuriated by the apostles' claims, the Sanhedrin members are ready to execute every apostle immediately. But one member of the Sanhedrin, Gamaliel, a respected teacher and a Pharisee, orders the apostles be dismissed from the room. Gamaliel then comes to their defense and reminds the Sanhedrin of two past attempted revolutions in Israel. He reasons that the historical incidents failed because God was not behind them. He argues that the Christian movement will also fail if God is not in it, but, if He is, they will find themselves fighting against Him. His persuasive presentation and the Sanhedrin's fear of mob action by people sympathetic to the apostles convince them to release the apostles once more.

The apostles are not released without punishment, however; they endure 39 brutal lashes. The Sanhedrin again orders the apostles to end their campaign for the hated Galilean. As the apostles leave the temple precincts, they rejoice that they have been permitted to suffer for the cause of Christ.

Personalize this lesson.

☑ The disciples rejoiced because they were counted worthy to suffer *"for the name"*! As we talk about Jesus, we, too, may suffer misunderstandings, rejection, discrimination, or worse. But God promises, *"After you have suffered a little while, the God of all grace … will Himself restore, confirm, strengthen, and establish you"* (1 Peter 5:8-11). If you are currently experiencing difficulty because you proclaim Jesus, thank Him for the opportunity to suffer for His name. Whether or not you are suffering for Him now, thank Him for His promise in 1 Peter 5.

Bridges for the Church
Acts 6–7

Memorize God's Word: Philippians 1:21.

❖ Acts 6:1-7—Meeting the Needs of the Church

1. What specific problem do the disciples face?

   _____

   _____

2. What are the qualifications of the men who distribute food to the needy?

   _____

   _____

   _____

3. What do you learn from this division of labor?

   _____

   _____

❖ Acts 6:8-15—Stephen Before the Sanhedrin

4. Using Acts 6:8-15, write a description of Stephen's character and attributes.

   _____

   _____

   _____

   _____

5. Read Matthew 10:19-20 and Luke 12:11-12. Explain why the men opposing Stephen could not overpower his wisdom and the Spirit with which he spoke.

_____

_____

6. According to the above verses and Acts 1:8, should Stephen's wisdom and boldness be considered unique? Why or why not?

_____

_____

7. What charges do these men make against Stephen?

_____

_____

❖ Acts 7:1-50—Stephen's Defense Recounts Jewish History

8. Read Acts 7:2-8 and Hebrews 11:8-19. Who was Abraham, according to these verses?

_____

_____

_____

9. What was the purpose of Joseph's suffering in Egypt, according to Genesis 50:18-21?

_____

_____

10. From Acts 7:17-29, describe Moses' background.

_____

_____

11. From Hebrews 11:23-29, what was the key to Moses' success?

_____

_____

12. How did the Israelites respond to Moses when he wanted to give them the living oracles of God (Acts 7:37-43)?

_____

_____

13. What were some of the consequences of their decision?

_____

_____

14. Read Acts 7:37 and Acts 3:20-23. Who was the Prophet whom Moses prophesied would come?

_____

_____

15. How does Stephen answer the charge that he is guilty of blaspheming God?

_____

_____

16. From Acts 7:44-50, how does Stephen answer the charge that he spoke words against the temple?

_____

_____

❖ Acts 7:51-60—Stephen Concludes His Speech and Is Stoned

17. In verse 51, why does Stephen tell the council they are *"stiff-necked"* and *"uncircumcised in hearts and ears"*? (See also Romans 2:28-29; Colossians 2:9-14.)

_____

_____

18. What causes them to be this way?

_____

_____

19. Reread verses 54-59, and note that almost every pronoun is plural. The action recorded here is carried out by a crowd of people. What are the dangers of going along with the crowd?

_____

_____

_____

20. What do Stephen's last moments on earth tell you about his relationship with God and his attitude toward death?

_____

_____

_____

21. What do you find most moving in this account?

_____

_____

_____

_____

Apply what you have learned. Stephen displayed an impressive knowledge of the Scriptures in his speech to the Sanhedrin. He showed his accusers that he had a thorough grasp of their religious heritage. Think about some individual whom you would like to know Jesus. What do you know about their current beliefs? Choose one action you could take this week to better understand their spiritual background, so that you can better explain the gospel in terms they will understand.

Bridges for the Church
Acts 6–7

Meeting the Needs of a Growing Church

As the church grows, it experiences difficulties revolving around a social issue. Peter and the disciples (a word used first in Acts as a general name for followers of Jesus) find ministering to the needs of a rapidly growing community overwhelming. A group of Hellenists— Greek-speaking Jews, now followers of Jesus—complain because their widows are being neglected in the church's daily distribution of food. In the 1st century, widows had no means of livelihood; many of them were in need.

The apostles bring the matter before the congregation. They ordain seven well-qualified Greek men to handle food distribution and support the apostles' preaching, teaching, and counseling work. We now see the growing church becoming organized. In addition, the progress report in Acts 6:7 records the spread of the Word, an increased number of disciples, and the conversion of priests. The statement *"a great many of the priests became obedient to the faith"* (6:7) is significant. About 8,000 priests and 10,000 Levites live in Jerusalem and the surrounding area. When so many become Christians, undoubtedly the leaders of the temple feel increasingly uneasy.

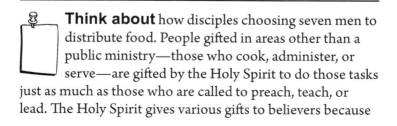

Think about how disciples choosing seven men to distribute food. People gifted in areas other than a public ministry—those who cook, administer, or serve—are gifted by the Holy Spirit to do those tasks just as much as those who are called to preach, teach, or lead. The Holy Spirit gives various gifts to believers because there are many ways to serve God. *"To each is given the manifestation of the Spirit for the common good"* (1 Corinthians 12:7).

Introducing Stephen

Luke describes Stephen as *"full of grace and power"* (Acts 6:8). A gifted, Spirit-filled man and brilliant preacher, he has great courage and faith. Through him, God works many signs and wonders. Out of this young, dedicated believer's life flow mighty preaching and enlightening instruction. However, Stephen is charged with blasphemy. Apparently, Stephen has been preaching faith in Jesus Christ, implying that the object of faith is God—not the Law, the temple, or Moses.

Stephen's Defense

The mob drags Stephen before the Sanhedrin. The high priest asks him if the charges of blasphemy are true. In the longest address in the Bible, Stephen responds by reviewing Israel's history. In apostolic times, the response of the accused was often a defense of the cause he supported rather than of himself. Stephen considers Israel's history to be a story of the acts of God. He recounts God's call of Abraham in Mesopotamia and His promise of land, numerous descendants, and special blessing. Yet neither Abraham nor the next two generations (Isaac and Jacob) inherited the land promised to them. Hundreds of years after Abraham's death, the land was given to the Israelites after their exile in Egypt. Stephen makes the point that without land, temple, or Law, God established His own chosen people.

Think about how Stephen's defense shows his knowledge of the Old Testament. According to Matthew 10:19-20 and Luke 12:11-12, the Holy Spirit will empower believers to speak when they are called to answer for their faith. However, we are still responsible to prepare and to study. *"The Holy Spirit … will teach you all things and bring to your remembrance all that I have said to you"* (John 14:26).

Stephen speaks of Joseph, showing Israel's rejection of those whom God sent to deliver them. Jews were proud of their link to the patriarchs, but it was the patriarchs who sold Joseph into slavery. God rescued Joseph and all Israel, yet the patriarchs died without possessing the Promised Land. Jacob was buried in Hebron in a cave bought from Ephron, the Hittite. Joseph and his brothers were buried in Shechem in Samaria. The Sanhedrin probably would not like to be reminded that the patriarchs possessed only unhallowed ground.

The next part of Stephen's defense proves to be the sharpest attack of all and the heart of his message. Like Joseph, Moses was rejected by his people, the Israelites. God called Moses to lead Israel out of Egypt and receive the Law on Mount Sinai. While Moses was on the mountain, face to face with the Living God, His chosen people made a shrine to the calf-headed Hathor (or Moloch), a popular Egyptian god. To Stephen, this idolatry was the crucial turning point in Israel's history. The rejection of Moses marked the beginning of the rejection of God Himself. Their nation's history became a story of intermittent rebellion interlaced with warnings from the prophets God sent to them.

Finally, Stephen tells of David's wish to build a *"dwelling place for the God of Jacob"* (Acts 7:46), a dream that Solomon fulfilled. Then he reminds the people that God does not dwell in houses made by hands. By emphasizing the acts of God outside the Holy Land, Stephen refutes the idea many Jews held that God's real presence could only be found within the temple walls in Jerusalem. He hints at a New Testament truth: Christ Himself is the dwelling place of the Most High.

The Stoning

Stephen's words are more likely a lament than an attack. He is moved by the realization that God's people throughout their history had been a *"stiff-necked people, uncircumcised in heart and ears"* (7:51). Their rebellion and refusal of God's offer in Jesus are really resistance to the Holy Spirit. He tells his accusers that he sees a vision of Jesus at God's right hand. Infuriated, the leaders stir up the mob. The people grab Stephen and drag him outside the city. Blasphemy is the charge; death by stoning is the sentence. As they stone him, Stephen prays for his persecutors. Before dying, he cries out, *"Lord, do not hold this sin against them"* (7:60).

Personalize this lesson.

Stephen, a man full of the Holy Spirit, was put to death for faithfulness to his Lord. As you read his story, which of his qualities do you most admire? Ask God to give you practical steps to take to develop this quality in your life. For example, if you admire Stephen's courage, He might lead you to memorize Psalm 56:3 and to step out of your comfort zone and do something that frightens you, trusting that He will keep you safe. Or, if you admire Stephen's command of Scripture, God may lead you to read and study a book of the Bible that is unfamiliar to you. You can be sure that Stephen didn't become the man he was automatically. He had to listen to God with a humble heart and let God train and empower him—just as we do.

Expansion Under Fire
Acts 8

Memorize God's Word: Isaiah 53:5.

❖ Acts 8:1-3—Persecution of the Jerusalem Believers

1. What happens to the believers in Jerusalem the day Stephen is stoned?

   _____

2. What connection do you see between this occurrence and Jesus' statement in Acts 1:8?

   _____

   _____

3. Read John 15:18–16:4. Why do you think people oppose the message of Jesus Christ and those who deliver it? Try to list at least five reasons.

   _____

   _____

   _____

   _____

   _____

4. How does Jesus prepare His disciples for such opposition, and what does this tell you about Him?

   _____

   _____

5. In the midst of this persecution, how did Stephen's friends handle his death?

    _____

    _____

6. What about can you learn from them about dealing with grief?

    _____

    _____

7. According to this text, what kind of man is Saul?

    _____

    _____

❖ Acts 8:4-8—Philip Goes to Samaria

8. As the believers scatter, what do they do, and what does this tell you about their faith?

    _____

    _____

9. Have you ever spoken to someone about Christ and experienced opposition? If so, what was your response?

    _____

    _____

10. Why do the Samaritans listen to Philip? Try to find at least two reasons.

    _____

    _____

    _____

    _____

11. What are the results of Philip's visit to Samaria?

    _____

    _____

❖ Acts 8:9-25—Philip Meets Simon the Magician

12. What can you learn about Simon's personality, work, religious background, and his response to the gospel?

_____

_____

_____

13. What do you think Peter means by his statement, *"Your heart is not right before God"* (verse 21)?

_____

_____

14. Have you ever done ministry with impure motives? What do you learn from this passage that might help you with that?

_____

_____

_____

_____

❖ Acts 8:26-29—God Sends Philip to an Ethiopian Eunuch

15. What is the spiritual condition of the Ethiopian eunuch at the time Philip approaches him?

_____

_____

16. How does God respond to this man?

_____

_____

17. What does Proverbs 2:1-5 promise about seeking God?

_____

_____

18. What does Jeremiah 29:13 promise about seeking God?

_____

19. What do you think it means to seek God? For help, consider the example of the Ethiopian eunuch and use a dictionary to define the word *seek*.

_____

_____

❖ Acts 8:30-40—The Ethiopian Eunuch Responds to Philip's Message

20. What encouragement can you find in John 14:26 and John 16:13-14, both in understanding Scripture and in sharing it with others as Philip did?

_____

_____

21. What can you learn from Philip's example about sharing Christ with others?

_____

_____

Apply what you have learned. As Philip devoted himself to telling people about Christ, God led him to a man who was seeking spiritual truth. Have you ever asked God to give you a "divine appointment"? Why not ask Him this week and then be ready! See who He leads you to, and then depend on Him to tell you the words to say and the things to do to share Jesus with that person.

Expansion Under Fire
Acts 8

The Seed of the Church

Stephen's martyrdom is one of several turning points in the progress of the gospel. His message causes the first general persecution of the church, which sends many believers running from Jerusalem, becoming refugees in surrounding Judea and nearby Samaria. Yet, instead of crushing the church, the persecution against Christians living in and around the Holy City *extends* the Christian community. Jerusalem is no longer the only city with a Christian church.

After a time, the apostles will also leave Jerusalem, but the Twelve remain there for now. The expanding church needs a home base, at least until newly formed congregations in other areas can stabilize and care for themselves. The apostles must stay in Jerusalem to minister to the believers who remain.

Many people mourn Stephen, but Saul is not one of them. To him, worshiping Jesus as Stephen had done was open blasphemy. According to Saul, the entire church is guilty of that same sin, so he systematically and vigorously attacks the Christians, literally making a door-to-door search. He takes the men and women he finds directly to jail.

Philip Goes Ahead

The Christians who escape the outbreak of persecution take seriously their Master's directive to make disciples. Philip goes to Samaria, the area between Judea on the south and Galilee on the north. He experiences a fruitful ministry in this land, despite the hostility between the Jews and Samaritans. The Samaritans, originally Jews of the northern kingdom of Israel, intermarried with settlers placed in their land during the Assyrian conquest in 722 BC. The Judean Jews considered the racially mixed Samaritans inferior.

Philip boldly proclaims that the Messiah had come, and signs and wonders witness to the truth of the gospel he preaches. As Samaritans express their faith, he receives them into the church. Simon the Magician is among those who hear Philip's testimony. Simon had convinced the Samaritans he possessed divine powers, and his practice of magic gathered a considerable following, but Philip's appearance challenges his reputation. As Simon listens to Philip preach, he decides he wants to be baptized.

Inspectors From Jerusalem

The apostles remaining in Jerusalem consider themselves authorities on church matters. When they learn the Samaritans *"received the word of God"* (Acts 8:14) and were baptized, they send Peter and John to investigate.

The Samaritans had been baptized only in the name of the Lord Jesus, so the apostles *"laid their hands on them and they received the Holy Spirit"* (8:17). At first, this explanation that the Samaritans believed in Jesus without receiving the indwelling Holy Spirit seems to contradict other parts of Scripture that teach we receive the Holy Spirit when we receive Christ. However, the book of Acts is a historical book about a transitional time in the life of the infant church, not a teaching book in the sense that Paul's letters are, for example. Therefore, it is possible God did something He has not repeated. From the text, we understand that external signs were visible when the Samaritans received the Holy Spirit, as they had been at Pentecost. Perhaps this special evidence was necessary for the Samaritans and the apostles to accept that these "despised outsiders" had indeed been fully received into the community of believers.

Whichever explanation you accept, their experience drew those early believers together in unity and solidarity. In the book of Acts, Luke proclaims that the Holy Spirit, long prophesied and expected, is bringing renewal to the world. He still comes to Jews, Samaritans, and Gentiles— to anyone of any race or nation who will repent and confess faith in Jesus.

Simon believes, but his growth and understanding are limited. His motive for wanting God's power and his method for acquiring it are all wrong. Peter responds with contempt to Simon's offer of money for spiritual power. He emphasizes that a person's heart must be right before God. He encourages Simon to repent, and Simon responds by asking Peter to pray for him.

As Peter and John return to Jerusalem, they preach the word of grace through Samaria.

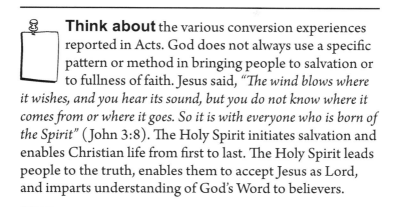

Think about the various conversion experiences reported in Acts. God does not always use a specific pattern or method in bringing people to salvation or to fullness of faith. Jesus said, *"The wind blows where it wishes, and you hear its sound, but you do not know where it comes from or where it goes. So it is with everyone who is born of the Spirit"* (John 3:8). The Holy Spirit initiates salvation and enables Christian life from first to last. The Holy Spirit leads people to the truth, enables them to accept Jesus as Lord, and imparts understanding of God's Word to believers.

God Sends Philip to Ethiopia

Through an angel, the Lord tells Philip to go south to Gaza, where the desert road joins the caravan route coming from the north. As Philip walks, a chariot passes carrying a man reading aloud. The man, an Ethiopian eunuch, serves as a court official to the Ethiopian queen. Then the Spirit says to Philip, *"Go over and join this chariot"* (Acts 8:29). Philip obeys and hears the man reading Isaiah 53. Philip asks him, *"Do you understand what you are reading?"* The man responds, *"How can I, unless someone guides me?"* (8:30-31). The Ethiopian then invites Philip to sit with him. As they ride along, Philip answers his questions. Philip then reveals to him that the Suffering Servant of Isaiah is Jesus, the Christ. And the Ethiopian—a man of another race and culture—believes!

As they ride along, they come to some water, and the Ethiopian asks Philip if he can be baptized. Philip baptizes him, and as they are coming out of the water, the Spirit of the Lord takes Philip away. The man goes on his way rejoicing, returning to his country as perhaps one of its first Christians. Philip continues his missionary efforts in Azotus and preaches the gospel in the towns there until he reaches Caesarea.

Personalize this lesson.

God is big enough to turn what seems like a disaster into something good. As the believers flee from persecution, they bring the gospel to new areas, and many trust Jesus. Have you ever seen God turn something that seemed bad at first into greater opportunity for ministry? If so, take a few minutes to reflect on that time and thank Him for how He worked. If you are experiencing a difficult situation right now, ask Him to show you some of the ways He may be using this experience for your good and the furthering of His kingdom. Thank God for His creative and redemptive power and ask Him to help you trust Him as He works out His plans.

Saul's Dramatic Conversion
Acts 9:1-30

❖ Acts 9:1-2—Saul, Who Became Paul

1. Read Acts 7:58; 8:1; 9:1-2; 22:20; and 26:9-11. What is Saul's attitude toward Jesus and those who believe in Him?

_____

_____

_____

_____

2. Why do you think Saul's persecution of the church is so intense? Try to suggest several reasons.

_____

_____

_____

_____

3. What is the new title given to the believers in 9:2?

_____

_____

4. Do you think this title is appropriate? Why or why not?

_____

_____

_____

_____

❖ Acts 9:3-9—Saul Encounters Christ on the Way to Damascus

5. Read Acts 22:6-11 and 26:12-18 along with Acts 9:3-9. What do you consider to be most remarkable about Saul's experience with Christ?

_____

_____

_____

_____

6. What can you learn about God's character from His conversation with Saul?

_____

_____

_____

7. According to the Scripture passages in question 5, who is Saul actually persecuting?

_____

❖ Acts 9:10-19—Saul and Ananias Meet in Damascus

8. How does Ananias's obedience progress as God commands him to go to Saul?

_____

_____

9. What impresses you most about Ananias?

_____

_____

10. How can you grow in this area?

_____

_____

11. From Acts 9:15-16, what is God's ministry for Saul?

_____

_____

12. Read 2 Corinthians 11:23–12:10. What different kinds of suffering does Paul experience?

_____

_____

_____

13. How does God bless Saul during this time?

_____

_____

❖ Acts 9:20-25—Saul's Preaching Triggers Jewish Opposition

14. Why do you think Saul is so eager to speak about Jesus?

_____

_____

15. What two truths does Saul preach in Damascus?

_____

_____

_____

16. What kind of emotions might Saul have experienced in Damascus?

_____

_____

❖ Acts 9:26-30—Saul Visits Jerusalem

17. What does Barnabas's name mean (Acts 4:36)?

_____

_____

18. What risks and sacrifices are involved in Barnabas's helping Saul, and what are the results?

_____

_____

_____

_____

19. Have you known a Christian who has been a personal encouragement to you? If so, what were the results of that encouragement?

_____

_____

_____

_____

20. Write the names of a few people God has placed in your life for you to encourage on a regular basis and the specific ways you can encourage them. Ask God to make you a more effective and consistent encourager.

_____

_____

_____

_____

_____

Apply what you have learned. Before his conversion to Christ, Saul was the Lord's hostile, headstrong opponent. Are there people like Saul in your life? How does the miracle of his conversion encourage you? No one is beyond God's reach. Think of one person who seems especially unlikely to follow Jesus, and commit to pray for him or her.

Saul's Dramatic Conversion
Acts 9:1-30

Saul was born in Tarsus, a city in the Roman province of Cilicia. His parents probably named him after Israel's first king and gave him a strong religious upbringing. Luke uses *Saul*, the Hebrew form of Paul's name, until Acts 13:9 where he writes, *"Saul, who was also called Paul."* When in Jerusalem, the apostle is called by his Hebrew name; while on evangelistic missions in Gentile areas, he is called Paul, the Roman form of his name. Paul wrote 13 of the 27 New Testament books. Although he greatly influenced the theology and evangelistic practices of the Christian church, during his lifetime he was unknown beyond his immediate area. Even Josephus, the major historian of the day, does not refer to him in his writings.

On the Road to Damascus

What Saul heard and saw on the day Stephen was martyred undoubtedly affected him for the rest of his life. Saul had viewed Stephen as a member of a dangerous new sect that was posing a threat to the Jewish faith. After Stephen's death, Saul persecutes other members of the Way. Upon learning that many have fled to Damascus, he obtains letters of arrest from the high priest and sets off to get rid of the hated "heretics."

As Saul and his company near Damascus, suddenly a blinding shaft of light causes him to fall to the ground. A voice calls, *"Saul, Saul, why are you persecuting Me?"* Saul responds, *"Who are You, Lord?"* The answer is as unexpected as the encounter: *"I am Jesus, whom you are persecuting"* (9:4-5). Saul thought he had been persecuting heretics and blasphemers, but he was actually persecuting Jesus, who identifies with His followers.

Saul's companions hear the sound and see the blinding light, but they do not or cannot understand it. Proud Saul, shocked and sightless, has to be led like a child into Damascus. During the next three days and nights he remains blind and does not eat or drink. What emotions he must have felt during those days of blindness!

Luke considers Saul's conversion experience central to the message of the book of Acts; he records two other accounts of it in his letter to Theophilus. Paul sees it as the core event in his life: *"You have heard of my former life in Judaism, how I persecuted the church of God violently and tried to destroy it. … But … He who had set me apart before I was born, and who called me by His grace, was pleased to reveal His Son to me, in order that I might preach Him among the Gentiles"* (Galatians 1:13-16).

Think about Paul's conversion as the beginning of his new life in Christ. Paul recounted the amazing event often to explain his changed life and to give glory to God. The apostle Peter wrote about *"always being prepared to make a defense to everyone who asks you for a reason for the hope that is in you"* (1 Peter 3:15). Are you prepared to talk about how you came to believe?

The Reluctant Brother

Damascus in Syria had a large Jewish community. The gospel had already reached the area, possibly through Jews in that city who had been converted in Jerusalem at Pentecost. Little is known of the background of the Jewish believer named Ananias. He was held in high regard by the Jews in Damascus (Acts 22:12) and may have been a Damascus native or a refugee from the persecution following the death of Stephen.

In a vision, the Lord directs Ananias to visit Saul of Tarsus, who is staying at Judas's home on the street called *Straight*. (Dating from before the days of Abraham, Damascus today is the oldest city in the world still in existence; Straight Street continues to be its main east-west artery.) God tells Ananias that Saul, still blind from his encounter with Jesus, is praying. The Lord reveals that Saul has seen a vision in which Ananias places his hands on him and restores his sight.

Ananias has heard of Saul and the suffering he has brought to the believers in Jerusalem. He lays his doubts and fears before God. Assured that going to Saul is God's will, he sets off to find him. Ananias greets him by laying his hands on him and calling him *"Brother Saul"* (9:17). He tells Saul he will not only regain his sight but also be filled with the Holy Spirit, and something like scales fall from Saul's eyes. He is then baptized as a believer in Christ.

Think about Ananias's relationship with Christ. The Lord addressed him by name, and his response was quick: *"Here I am, Lord"* (9:10). In simple faith, Ananias received the Lord's instructions, then followed them. Although he may have had some inner qualms, he acted graciously, addressing Saul as *"Brother Saul"* (9:17). Ananias's obedience allowed him to play a small but crucial role in the advance of the gospel.

Many Directions

Saul's direction changes, but his zeal and energy remain the same. Saul immediately starts preaching in the Damascus synagogues, boldly declaring Jesus as the Son of God. What a testimony to the power of God's Spirit to change lives! Saul begins a pattern in Damascus that characterizes his lifelong missionary enterprise: He goes to the synagogues and uses Old Testament Scriptures to show the Jews that Jesus is the long-awaited Messiah and the Son of God.

Orthodox Jews as well as Jews who become followers of Jesus live in Damascus. To the second group, Saul's preaching is supportive; to the first group, his conversion is the final insult. These Jews plot to kill him, posting guards at the city gates, but Saul's disciples help him escape, lowering him through an opening in the city wall.

Saul returns to Jerusalem, but the believers there are suspicious of him. However, Barnabas becomes Saul's sponsor, taking him to the apostles and testifying to the validity of his Damascus experience. Saul again begins to witness boldly in the name of Christ. Trouble with the Hellenists arises, and as opposition grows, it seems Stephen's death by stoning may be repeated. Saul's friends decide to get him out of town. By way of Caesarea, he travels to Tarsus in Cilicia, his birthplace.

Personalize this lesson.

✓ Luke wrote a highly compressed account of Paul's conversion. Paul says that he *"went away into Arabia, and returned again to Damascus. Then after three years* [he] *went up to Jerusalem"* (Galatians 1:17-18.) God is not in a hurry. The great apostle Paul had to wait for years to begin his ministry. God works in our lives on His timetable. What are you waiting for God to do in, for, or through you? How do you do with waiting? If you need encouragement while you wait on God, consider doing a Bible study on the occurrences of "wait" in Psalms. What verses challenge you? What verses give you hope? Ask God to give you a patient and trusting heart so that you can fully embrace His timing.

You Are Peter, the Rock
Acts 9:31-11:18

❖ **Acts 9:31-43—Aeneas Is Healed, and Dorcas Is Brought Back to Life**

1. How does Luke describe the church throughout Judea, Galilee, and Samaria (9:31)? What aspect of his description most stands out to you and why?

    _____

    _____

    _____

2. What is wrong with Aeneas, and how long has he been this way?

    _____

    _____

3. How is he healed?

    _____

    _____

4. How would you describe the kind of woman Dorcas was?

    _____

    _____

5. What does Peter do when he goes to the house where Dorcas's body lies?

    _____

    _____

6. What are the results of this miracle?

_____

_____

❖ Acts 10:1-22—Cornelius Sends for Peter

7. How is Cornelius an illustration of the kind of seeker of God described in Hebrews 11:6?

_____

_____

8. How does God reward Cornelius?

_____

_____

9. How would you describe Peter's vision? Include details.

_____

_____

10. Read Leviticus 11:1-31 (especially verses 1-4, 9-10, 13, 24-25), and explain why you think Peter refuses to eat the animals.

_____

_____

_____

_____

❖ Acts 10:17-33—Peter Visits Cornelius

11. Knowing how difficult it is for Peter to associate with Gentiles, God directs him to go to Cornelius in three different ways. What are they? (See also Acts 10:1-16.)

_____

_____

_____

_____

12. Both Peter and Cornelius practice hospitality. What basic attitudes are evident in their hospitality? Which attitude do you most want to emulate?

_____

_____

13. How does Peter relate the vision God gave him in Joppa to his visit with Cornelius?

_____

_____

14. Read 1 Peter 1:18-19 and 1 John 1:9 with Acts 10:14, 28. How does God cleanse a believer?

_____

_____

_____

_____

❖ Acts 10:34-48—God Gives the Holy Spirit to Gentile Believers

15. Peter's sermon in verses 34-43 is important because it is the first sermon in the Bible preached exclusively to Gentiles. What are the main points of the sermon, and what does each one mean to you?

_____

_____

_____

_____

16. How does God reveal to the believing Jews and Gentiles that His salvation is for Gentile and Jew alike?

_____

_____

_____

❖ Acts 11:1-18—Jewish Believers in Jerusalem Accept Gentile Believers

17. How does Peter deal with the criticism from the Jewish Christians in Jerusalem?

_____

_____

18. What can you learn from Peter about facing criticism?

_____

_____

19. How does Peter's audience respond to this explanation of being with the Gentiles and eating with them?

_____

_____

20. Compare 2 Corinthians 7:10 with Acts 11:18. What do you think *"repentance that leads to life"* means?

_____

_____

_____

_____

Apply what you have learned. God showed Peter that no group of people was "unclean," that he could associate with anyone, and that the gospel was for everyone. Most of us tend to avoid people unlike ourselves: those who are richer or poorer, more or less educated, younger or older, etc. This week, strike up a conversation with someone you perceive to be unlike you. Try to talk with that person until you find something in common. Talk with God about what you learn from this experience.

You Are Peter, the Rock
Acts 9:31-11:18

A Time of Peace

Luke ties the book of Acts together in 9:31: *"The church throughout all Judea and Galilee and Samaria had peace and was being built up. And walking in the fear of the Lord and in the comfort of the Holy Spirit, it multiplied."* The word *church* describes the entire group of believers—the combined congregations from all areas. What does it mean that the church had peace? Persecutions continued; Roman armies marched. Still the church was at peace, a result of the Holy Spirit's encouragement. Isaiah 26:3 promises, *"You keep him in perfect peace whose mind is stayed on You, because he trusts in You."*

Saul was in Arabia (Galatians 1:17) being taught by the Holy Spirit for the task ahead of him. Missionaries spread the good news of Christ, and people in Judea, Galilee, and Samaria found new hope. Thousands surrendered to God, and the church continued in peace. God planned to expand the church beyond Israel's borders; this was a time of preparation. In Jerusalem, Peter and the apostles were growing in the knowledge of God and in spiritual wisdom and understanding. The local church was multiplying and maturing. The Lord was preparing for an explosion of the church universal.

Think about Jesus' statement to His disciples: *"Peace I leave with you; My peace I give to you. Not as the world gives do I give to you. Let not your hearts be troubled, neither let them be afraid"* (John 14:27). The peace of God differs from any other kind of peace because God's peace does not depend on our circumstances but on our faith in Him.

We have the assurance that we are secure in God's love and care regardless of what is happening (or may happen) in the world.

Peter's First Pastoral Visits

As Peter begins to minister outside Jerusalem, God enables him to perform signs and wonders. He visits cities along the Mediterranean coast where Philip had established congregations. Of the cities Peter visited, Luke mentions Lydda, Joppa, and Caesarea. Luke refers to the believers in Lydda as *"saints"* (Acts 9:13, 32). Saints in the Christian context include *"all who have believed"* (2 Thessalonians 1:10).

Peter encounters Aeneas, a paralyzed man of Lydda who has been bedridden for eight years. Peter calls his name and says, *"Jesus Christ heals you; rise and make your bed"* (Acts 9:34). Aeneas gets up at once, completely healed.

In the nearby seaport of Joppa lives a Christian named Tabitha, also known as Dorcas, who becomes ill and dies. Disciples send for Peter, who sends all the mourners out of the room. Then he prays, tells the woman to rise, and she sits up. Dorcas's restoration is the first instance of a disciple raising someone from the dead. Many people come to faith in Christ because of these miracles.

Peter Visits Cornelius

Peter remains in Joppa for some time at Simon the tanner's home. Because the Jews considered tanning an unclean occupation, Peter's decision to stay with Simon indicates how much he has grown spiritually. While at Simon's house, Peter sees a vision of a great sheet filled with all types of animals, reptiles, and birds, clean and unclean according to Levitical Law. Peter hears a voice commanding him to *"kill and eat"* (Acts 10:13) but refuses in obedience to dietary laws. The Lord replies, *"What God has made clean, do not call common"* (10:15). Then, the Holy Spirit informs him that three men are looking for him. On the previous day, God visited Cornelius, a Roman centurion. An angel of God assured Cornelius of God's favor and told him to send for Peter. When Peter arrives, Cornelius bows and "worships" him, but Peter gently stops him, insisting he is only a man. Seeing the relatives and friends Cornelius has assembled, Peter states that he is there by direct revelation of God. Cornelius responds with sensitivity and insight.

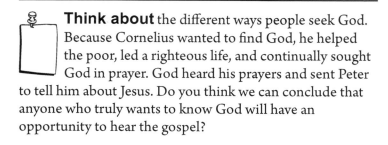 **Think about** the different ways people seek God. Because Cornelius wanted to find God, he helped the poor, led a righteous life, and continually sought God in prayer. God heard his prayers and sent Peter to tell him about Jesus. Do you think we can conclude that anyone who truly wants to know God will have an opportunity to hear the gospel?

Peter Preaches to the Gentiles

Peter's sermon, the first sermon preached to Gentiles, presents a clear message: God shows no partiality; He has His people in every race and nation and accepts anyone who fears Him and does what is right. Peter then states essential facts about Jesus: All Old Testament prophecies were fulfilled in Him, and every person may receive forgiveness in His name. At this point, an outpouring of the Holy Spirit occurs. The Jewish believers' doubts about the Gentiles' entrance into God's kingdom vanish. Peter commands them to be baptized in the name of Jesus Christ and brought into the fellowship of the church.

Peter Justifies His Daring Act

The Jerusalem church held that anyone who had been circumcised and accepted the Law of Moses, including Gentiles, could become a member of the church. When the full story of what had happened in Caesarea reaches Jerusalem, the circumcised believers criticize Peter for staying and eating with uncircumcised Gentiles. Peter defends himself by relating what had occurred, starting with the vision from God and His clear instructions to go with Cornelius's men. Six witnesses from Joppa go with Peter and also testify that God has given the gift of the Holy Spirit to the Gentiles, a visible sign of His acceptance. Peter concludes that he could not oppose God. Peter's testimony silences his critics—for a time.

Personalize this lesson.

☑ God doesn't show favoritism. Everyone who has made a simple declaration of faith in Jesus as Savior is a child of God. Yet there are many ways to follow Jesus and express faith in Him. As you think about believers in your community and around the world who worship and live differently from you, examine your heart. Are you ever tempted to look down on those whose traditions, music, dress, type of worship service, etc., is different from yours? If so, consider trying this little experiment. Is there a Christian church in your community that is very different from the church traditions you are comfortable in? Plan to go there to worship this weekend, or one weekend soon. Instead of looking to see what they do "wrong," ask God to show you what He enjoys about the way they worship and serve Him. As you learn, thank Him for the rich variety He has created in His church.

The Founding of a Church
Acts 11:19-12:25

Memorize God's Word: Luke 11:13.

❖ Acts 11:19-26—A Church Begins and Grows in Antioch

1. How does the church in Antioch begin and progress?

   _____

   _____

2. Realizing that no believers lived in Antioch prior to the arrival of the men from Cyprus and Cyrene, what do you find most interesting or challenging about the development of this church?

   _____

   _____

3. What does Barnabas see when he arrives in Antioch? What do you think this means?

   _____

   _____

4. What does Barnabas do in Antioch?

   _____

   _____

5. What does it mean to *"remain faithful to the Lord"* (11:23)?

   _____

   _____

6. What do Barnabas and Saul do for the believers in Antioch?

_____

_____

7. Why are meeting together and sound teaching still important for Christians today?

_____

_____

_____

❖ Acts 11:27-30—Agabus Predicts a Famine

8. What specific signs indicate Agabus was a true prophet (Deuteronomy 18:20-22)?

_____

_____

9. What facts can you discover about how the Christians in Antioch gave?

_____

_____

10. Which principles here might you apply to your giving now?

_____

_____

_____

❖ Acts 12:1-11—Herod Imprisons Peter and an Angel Releases Him

11. According to this text, what kinds of suffering do Christians experience at this time?

_____

_____

_____

12. Compare Acts 12:3 with John 12:42-43. Whom is Herod really trying to please?

    _____

    _____

    _____

13. What do the believers do when they hear Peter has been imprisoned? What seems to be the result?

    _____

    _____

14. What do the following verses say about prayer?

    a. Ephesians 6:18 _____

        _____

    b. Colossians 4:2 _____

        _____

    c. Matthew 7:7 _____

        _____

    d. James 4:2-3 _____

        _____

    e. James 5:16 _____

        _____

    f. 1 John 5:14 _____

        _____

    g. John 15:7 _____

        _____

15. In the verses above, which principle about prayer most challenges or encourages you? Based on these verses, how would you like to begin building a stronger prayer life?

    _____

    _____

    _____

❖ Acts 12:12-17—Peter Describes His Miraculous Release to His Friends

16. What do you find humorous, surprising, predictable, or unusual in Peter's reunion with his friends?

_____

_____

17. Why do you think Peter comes to see his friends?

_____

_____

18. Read Psalm 105:1-5. Using Peter as an example, what do you see as the value of sharing with others what God has done for you?

_____

_____

_____

❖ Acts 12:18-25—Herod's Death

19. Read verse 23 and Isaiah 42:8. What was Herod's sin?

_____

_____

20. How can people be guilty of that same sin today?

_____

_____

Apply what you have learned. The church offered *"earnest prayer"* for Peter's release from prison. God heard and answered in a miraculous way. Is there a situation in your life, or in the life of someone you know, that needs a miracle? Every day this week, ask God to intervene, remembering how He delivered Peter from prison.

The Founding of a Church
Acts 11:19-12:25

A Church Begins in Antioch

At last the gospel moves beyond Israel into Gentile territory. The church begins to grow in Antioch, the third largest city in the Roman Empire after Rome and Alexandria. In the 1st century AD, Antioch, as capital of Syria, was rich, sophisticated, and advanced in scientific achievement. But the people had a bad reputation, even by Roman standards, because of their association with the worship of the goddess Artemis, one of the most corrupt, immoral, polytheistic religious cults of that day.

Followers of Christ fleeing persecution in Jerusalem begin to share their newfound faith in Jesus with the Jews in Antioch. But believers from Cyprus and Cyrene in North Africa also preach Christ to Gentiles, who accept the gospel. When news of this reaches Jerusalem, the conservative church there is concerned and sends a well-respected member, Barnabas—a Levite from Cyprus, a good man, tolerant, and full of the Holy Spirit—to investigate. Barnabas sees what is occurring and rejoices, encouraging those new to the faith. As the work progresses, Barnabas needs help and remembers Saul, whom he had befriended earlier, and brings him from Tarsus to serve with him. Their ministry together continues for a year with outstanding results.

In Antioch, believers are first called *Christians*. The word literally means *those belonging to Christ*. The Antioch church crosses racial, cultural, and language barriers. Despite their differences, Christ unites them all so they are all *Christians*. From this time, the term *Christian* becomes the universal name for those who follow Christ.

First Christian Hunger Appeal

Certain individuals during the time of the early church were specially gifted by God's Spirit. The Antioch church receives a visit from a prophet named Agabus, who arrives from Jerusalem and predicts a worldwide famine. The famine occurs during the years AD 41–54. Judea experiences a severe drought in AD 46 and a bad harvest the following year. Crop failures in Egypt, a main source of grain in the Mediterranean, and limited production in Judea contribute to high prices and the scarcity of grain. Agabus's speech stirs the church in Antioch to send relief to the stricken city. The church commissions Paul and Barnabas to take the gift to the elders for distribution to the people in Jerusalem. The mention of elders furnishes a clue that the Jerusalem church was developing organizational structures.

Persecution Under Herod

The Roman Empire historically maintained control over diverse nations by giving power and prestige to local people they considered to be trustworthy. Loyalty to Rome was the first requirement for such a position. In Palestine, Roman authorities chose the Herodian family. Ethnically they were Edomites, descendants of Esau. Under Rome, they ruled intermittently from 37 BC to AD 70—a period characterized by cruelty toward and harassment of the Jews. Intrigue, intermarriage, murder, and bribery mark this infamous family's history. For instance, Herod Antipas the Tetrarch had John the Baptist beheaded for confronting him about marrying his brother's wife. Herod the Great ordered the death of baby boys in the Bethlehem vicinity at the time of Jesus' birth.

Always loyal to Rome, Herod Agrippa I, Herod Antipas's nephew, strengthens his position with Jewish leaders by executing James, the brother of John and a church leader. Herod's persecution of "heretics" delights the Jews. Pleased with their response, Herod arrests Peter. This persecution begins during Passover—the same time of year that Jesus' arrest had taken place. However, Herod plans no action during this Jewish high holiday because Jews would not want an execution at this time. Instead, he puts Peter in prison and keeps him heavily guarded. However, Herod has not counted on the power of intercessory prayer!

Peter's Farewell in Acts

The night before Peter's trial, an angel enters his cell and leads him out of the prison. Peter assumes he is seeing a vision until he finds himself alone in the street. He goes to a house where his friends are praying for him. The believers are surprised by Peter's release. Peter shares his experience with them, asks them to tell James (a relative of the Lord and a church leader) and the brothers, and then departs.

Think about the Christians praying for Peter's release. They had suffered much and didn't know what to expect from their earnest prayers. Peter's friends feared he might have already been killed, for when Rhoda brought the news that Peter was at the door, they thought she had seen *"his angel."* Many of us react with the same amazement and disbelief in response to answered prayer. God continues to surprise us today and often answers our prayers far more abundantly than we have dared to ask.

Herod's Death

Peter's disappearance has grim results. Herod learns of the empty cell and has the guards executed. (Roman law held the guard responsible with his own life if a prisoner escaped.) Herod then leaves Jerusalem for Caesarea. Few, if any, Jews live there, but Herod faces another problem. The Phoenician cities of Tyre and Sidon depend on the Roman Empire for food. Herod has levied a heavy tax on imported food, reasoning that the people of Tyre and Sidon can well afford to pay because they have become wealthy through trade. The citizens have asked for relief from the tax. When Herod speaks to them from his throne, they shout, *"The voice of a god, and not of a man!"* (12:22). Herod accepts their praise. Instantly, an angel of the Lord strikes him for not giving God the glory, and he is literally *"eaten by worms"* (Acts 12:23) and dies.

At this time, both Antioch and Jerusalem serve as centers of the church, but Antioch emerges as the center of missionary activity. Paul and Barnabas return from Jerusalem to Antioch with John Mark. Their time with the spiritually strong congregation at Antioch prepares them for their next step of faith—what we know as Paul's first missionary journey.

Personalize this lesson.

Barnabas exhorted the new believers in Antioch to *"remain faithful to the Lord with steadfast purpose."* Considering your response to question 5, prayerfully consider what it will take for you to remain faithful to God for a lifetime. What purposes has God given you? How can you avoid becoming distracted from your calling? What do you need from God, specifically, to help you remain steadfast in faith? Ask Him for that. He is more than able to help you!

New Frontiers
Acts 13

Memorize God's Word: Luke 11:13.

❖ Acts 13:1-12—The Church Commissions the First Missionaries

1. Who are the leaders in the Antioch church, and what are they doing when God speaks to them?

   _____

   _____

2. Who accompanies Paul and Barnabas?

   _____

3. Upon arriving in Salamis, what do Paul and Barnabas do?

   _____

   _____

4. Elymas the magician tries to turn the proconsul away from faith as Paul presents God's Word to him (13:8). How does Paul confront Elymas?

   _____

   _____

5. Why does the proconsul believe Paul's teaching?

   _____

   _____

❖ Acts 13:13-25—Paul Begins to Preach in Antioch of Pisidia

6. What pattern is Paul repeating here? (See also Acts 13:5 and Romans 1:16.)

_____

_____

7. As Paul summarizes Jewish history from God's perspective, what facts does he include?

_____

_____

8. Why do you think he chooses to recount their history in this way?

_____

_____

_____

9. Which of the facts about God in Paul's summary means the most to you, and why?

_____

_____

_____

❖ Acts 13:26-29—Paul Preaches About the Death of Jesus

10. According to the text, why did the Jerusalem Jews reject Jesus?

_____

_____

11. Why do you think people reject Jesus today?

_____

_____

_____

12. What does Paul emphasize about Jesus' death and the related events?

_____

_____

13. Why do you think Paul focuses on these specific details?

_____

_____

❖ Acts 13:30-43—Paul Preaches About the Resurrection

14. Who was responsible for Jesus' resurrection?

_____

_____

15. In His ministry, Jesus brought several people back from death to life. What does this Scripture say is different about Jesus' resurrection?

_____

_____

16. What do we receive as a result of Jesus' resurrection?

_____

_____

_____

17. What do we need to do to be forgiven?

_____

_____

_____

18. According to the following passages, name some benefits of being forgiven by God.

a. Psalm 32:1-5 _____

_____

b. Jeremiah 31:34 _____

_____

c. 1 John 1:9 _____

_____

19. According to verse 39, how is the benefit Jesus provided superior to what the law of Moses could do?

_____

_____

_____

❖ Acts 13:44-52—Gentiles Receive With Joy What Antioch Jews Reject

20. What makes the Jews jealous?

_____

_____

21. How do Paul and Barnabas respond to the Jews who drive them away? (See Matthew 10:11-15 for an explanation of what "[shaking] *the dust from their feet*" means.)

_____

_____

_____

Apply what you have learned. God gave Paul and Barnabas the courage to continually speak the truth and to persevere despite strong opposition on their first missionary journey. For what personal situation do you need to be filled with God's courage or perseverance? Every day this week, ask God for what you need, and then, in faith, act on it, regardless of your feelings.

New Frontiers
Acts 13

The church at Antioch is led by the Holy Spirit. No church officers are elected, but prophets and teachers are recognized for their spiritual gifts. Teaching instructs believers in God's Word so that they may grow in the Lord. Prophecy both (1) foretells future events—as when Agabus warns of the coming famine (Acts 11:28); and (2) speaks God's Word—as when the Holy Spirit gives individuals special insight into the Word to warn, enlighten, and encourage others.

The Birth of Missions

The Antioch congregation initiates three things that mark it as unique:

❖ It pioneers the breakdown of hostility between Jews and Gentiles.

❖ It is the first congregation to attempt to meet the needs of a less-fortunate sister church.

❖ By sending out Paul and Barnabas, it acts on the Lord's command to go into all the world and make disciples.

Luke names five spiritually gifted prophets and teachers in Acts 13:1. Barnabas and Saul, the oldest and youngest of the group, have already been introduced. The others are Manaen, a boyhood friend of Herod the Tetrarch; Lucius, from Cyrene in North Africa; and Simeon, called Niger, who may have helped Jesus carry His cross.

After praying, fasting, and sensing the Holy Spirit's direction, the Antioch church blesses Barnabas and Saul and sends them out. They travel to Seleucia, a seaport 16 miles west of Antioch, and then sail for the island of Cyprus (Barnabas's home territory). They land at Salamis, the chief commercial city on the island. Preaching in the synagogue before seeking out Gentiles, they set a pattern for future journeys. John Mark, Barnabas's cousin and Peter's student, accompanies them. Mark is not an apostle, but he probably assists Saul and Barnabas in teaching the basics of the faith to new converts. Traveling 90 miles across the island to the political capital of Paphos, the trio meets Sergius Paulus, the learned Roman proconsul who governs the island. His group includes a Jewish magician and false prophet named Elymas (also called Bar-Jesus). Elymas opposes Paul, who rebukes Elymas and causes him to experience temporary blindness. Impressed by Paul's teaching and the punishment of Elymas, the proconsul becomes a believer.

In verse 9, Luke changes the name *Saul* to *Paul* (his Roman name) as the team enters Gentile territory. In their commissioning, Barnabas's name comes before Saul's (13:2), but in the encounter with the magician, Saul steps forward and, *"filled with the Holy Spirit"* (13:9), takes charge. Verse 13 begins *"Paul and his companions,"* indicating a shift in authority and leadership.

When the missionaries leave Paphos, they sail 175 miles across the Mediterranean to Asia Minor, landing at Attalia, then going to Perga in the province of Pamphylia. At this point, John Mark leaves the group and returns to Jerusalem. Scholars suggest various reasons for Mark's departure: He is homesick; he is too young and immature; he has difficulty adjusting to the hostile climate; he is offended that Paul emerges as the apostolic leader, preferring Barnabas's leadership; or he does not like the mission's emphasis on Gentiles. Later on, Barnabas wants to give him a second chance.

Think about what we can learn from John Mark. Whatever his reason for leaving Paul and Barnabas, he did not fulfill his obligation. But when we disappoint others and walk away from our responsibilities, there is hope. Just as John Mark evidently matured and later reconciled with Paul, we, too, may ask for forgiveness and the chance to continue God's work. Remember that Mark, who once ran away from his duty, later wrote one of the Gospels.

Paul Preaches in Another Antioch

Paul's group now climbs the Taurus Mountains and reaches the plains of Anatolia, homeland of the Hittite and Phrygian civilizations. The Greeks had colonized the coastal cities but not the interior, and the Caesars did not Romanize the backlands until 100 years after Paul's time. Paul has reached a challenging mission field where the people worship local gods and speak many dialects.

In Pisidian Antioch, the missionaries go into the synagogue. The synagogue leaders recognize Paul as a Pharisee and an important guest whose remarks would be considered edifying. Paul's audience consists of *"Men of Israel* [orthodox Jews] *and you who fear God* [Gentiles]*"* (Acts 13:16). The first part of Paul's sermon resembles Stephen's speech in its overview of God's dealings with Israel. But while Stephen stressed Israel's rebelliousness, Paul's tone and content are milder. Paul begins the second part of his sermon by identifying with his hearers as *"brothers, sons of the family of Abraham,"* including also the Gentiles, whom he addresses as *"those among you who fear God"* (13:26). Then Paul speaks of Jesus' death and resurrection, using the Scriptures to demonstrate that Jesus is the Anointed One. In the final section of his message, Paul explains that all believers are justified by faith in Christ and given freedom that the Law of Moses could not give.

The Missionaries Turn to the Gentiles

Paul's words are well received, and the next Sabbath almost the whole city gathers to hear the Word of God. The synagogue leaders are jealous of Paul's enthusiastic reception. They contradict Paul's teaching and verbally attack him. Because the Jews reject the gospel message, the missionaries decide to concentrate on the Gentiles, fulfilling the prophecy in Isaiah 49:6: *"I will make You as a light for the nations, that My salvation may reach to the end of the earth."* Paul takes a new direction and marks a decisive moment in church development; until then, missionary efforts had been directed to the Jews. But now, converts with no commitment to Judaism will spread the gospel throughout the nations.

Personalize this lesson.

It is natural when we begin sharing our faith to begin with those who seem most likely to respond. If these people are not interested, it is also natural to give up. We may decide we are not gifted at talking about Jesus, or that people today just don't want to hear about Him. Instead of giving up when the Jews opposed him, Paul and company shifted their ministry to a group that seemed less likely to believe—and they became Christians!

If you have become discouraged in your attempts to talk about Jesus, ask the Lord to speak to you through this account. Confess any poor attitudes and ask God to give you a new desire to share the gospel with unbelievers. Pray that God will lead you to people who are open to His Word, even if they seem like unlikely candidates at first.

We Will Go to the Gentiles
Acts 14

❖ **Acts 14:1-7—Paul and Barnabas Preach the Gospel in Iconium**

1. What happened during Paul and Barnabas's stay in Iconium?

   _____

   _____

   _____

2. In spite of opposition, Paul and Barnabas continue to preach. What character qualities do you see in Paul and Barnabas?

   _____

   _____

   _____

3. What do the following verses say about facing difficulties in one's walk with Christ?

   a. 1 Corinthians 15:58 _____

   _____

   b. 2 Timothy 2:3-5 _____

   _____

   c. James 1:2-4_____

   _____

❖ Acts 14:8-18—Paul and Barnabas Minister in Lystra

4. What enables the lame man to walk? (See also Acts 3:16.)

_____

_____

5. How do the people of Lystra react to this miracle?

_____

_____

6. How do Paul and Barnabas respond to the crowds?

_____

_____

7. Paul and Barnabas are speaking to a Gentile audience here. How does this sermon differ from the sermon Paul preached to the Jews in Acts 13:16-41?

_____

_____

_____

8. What do you learn from Paul about witnessing?

_____

_____

_____

9. Compare Paul's sermon in this passage with Romans 1:18-25, and explain what God reveals through His creation.

_____

_____

_____

10. What evidence do we have today of the truth of this passage?

_____

_____

❖ Acts 14:19-23—Paul Is Stoned and Believed Dead

11. Why do you think the people in Lystra could turn away from Paul so easily, and what do you learn from this?

_____

_____

12. What difficult circumstances are you experiencing in your life? How could this incident from Paul's life encourage you?

_____

_____

_____

❖ Acts 14:21-23—Paul Returns to Cities He Previously Evangelized

13. Which of Jesus' commands do Paul and Barnabas fulfill in Derbe (Matthew 28:19)?

_____

_____

14. Paul and Barnabus return to Lystra, Iconium, and Antioch to strengthen the new believers there, even though people from these cities had tried to kill him. What does that say to you about the importance they place on nurturing young Christians in their faith?

_____

_____

15. In what ways do Paul and Barnabas minister to the disciples they visit? How might they have done each of these things?

_____

_____

16. What did you learn from Paul's example in this passage?

_____

_____

❖ Acts 14:24-28—Paul and Barnabas Return to Their Home Church in Antioch

17. What does this text say about the work Paul and Barnabas did on this journey?

_____

_____

_____

_____

18. What do Paul and Barnabas do when they return to Antioch?

_____

_____

19. How was this step beneficial both to Paul and Barnabas and the church in Antioch?

_____

_____

_____

_____

Apply what you have learned. Paul and Barnabas display amazing steadfastness in spite of opposition and discouragement. Unfortunately, such discouragement is often a part of ministry. Look up and write out several verses about perseverance. (Revisit the Scriptures in question 1, and look up words such as *steadfast*, *perseverance*, and *endure* in a concordance or online Bible reference.) Choose the verse that means the most to you and memorize it this week.

We Will Go to the Gentiles
Acts 14

In Pisidian Antioch, Paul preached his first recorded sermon. For the first—but not the last—time, he and Barnabas were run out of town because of the gospel message. (Paul was chased out of town almost as often as he left on his own!) As they left Pisidian Antioch, *"the disciples were filled with joy and with the Holy Spirit"* (Acts 13:52).

Testimony to Iconium

Paul and Barnabas head east to Iconium, a 90-mile journey through rolling hills and fertile plains. Iconium, the capital of the region, is the most important city Paul and Barnabas will visit on this extended trip, and Paul will return at least twice. One of the early church councils was held there. Now called Konia, the city still exists today.

Because Iconium has a sizable Jewish community, Paul first preaches in a synagogue. Paul and Barnabas work successfully among both Jews and Greeks. Apparently, the Greeks, called "God fearers," attend the synagogue, and the people respond favorably to the gospel message. Although unbelieving Jews still have enough influence in the town to prevent a surge of Christian growth, the apostles remain in town for *"a long time,"* speaking boldly. To confirm their message, God enables them to do *"signs and wonders."* Eventually, enemies of the apostles succeed in causing such division among the people that the situation grows dangerous. Gentile magistrates and the synagogue leaders mistreat Paul and Barnabas and finally decide to stone them—the punishment for blasphemy.

Undesired Honors in Lystra

When the apostles learn of the intended stoning, they flee 25 miles south to Lystra in Anatolia—not to rest but to preach the gospel. Lystra had few Jews and no synagogue. There Paul heals a man with crippled feet, an account similar to Peter's healing of a lame man in the Jerusalem temple (3:1-10). Luke, the physician, describes the condition of the lame man using details of interest to a doctor: He was *"crippled from birth and had never walked"* (14:8). The man listens intently as the apostle speaks. Looking directly at him, Paul observes that he has *"faith to be made well"* (14:9). Inspired by the Holy Spirit, Paul speaks the word that enables the man to spring up and walk.

In response to the miracle, the citizens shout, *"The gods have come down to us"* (14:11). From the Temple of Zeus in the front of the city, the priest hears the shouts and parades oxen out for sacrifice. The two apostles do not understand what the people are shouting because neither speaks the local dialect. But when the oxen appear, they realize they are being paid divine honors. They tear their clothes and rush into the crowd to protest.

Paul speaks either in Latin—the language of the Roman Empire—or through an interpreter. In his first speech given specifically to a Gentile audience, he portrays God as Lord of the universe and Giver of life. Rather than testifying about Jesus, He speaks of the oneness of God. He tells his audience that he and Barnabas are men, not gods, and explains that he is a messenger of Good News offered to all who turn from worthless things (like the pagan temple, altar, and statues) to Christ. His words barely restrain the people from offering sacrifices to them. Soon, enemies arrive from Antioch (100 miles away) and Iconium (20 miles away) and influence some of the people in Lystra, for a mob's emotions are easily swayed. They stone Paul, drag him from the city, and leave him for dead.

Think about why Paul and Barnabas faced persecution so often. On most occasions, Jewish leaders, jealous of the Jews and Gentiles' warm response to the gospel, sparked the persecution of those spreading the good news. Even Paul had once persecuted Christians. Jesus warned His disciples that they would be persecuted, and as a result, many would abandon their faith and betray one another (Matthew 24:9-10).

Throughout history, Christians have been persecuted. How can we be ready to face opposition to our faith?

The Work Goes On

The disciples, probably people who responded to the gospel in Iconium and Lystra, gather about Paul's seemingly lifeless body. But he is still alive! Paul remains in Lystra overnight and then, miraculously healed, goes to Derbe with Barnabas the next day, preaching and making many disciples. At this point, Paul and Barnabas could have turned south, easily reaching the town of Seleucia and the Mediterranean Sea. But Paul's heart is not drawn there. Having left Lystra, Iconium, and Pisidian Antioch quickly, he is eager to return to strengthen the believers there, knowing they, too, might face persecution one day. In Derbe, no persecution is mentioned. In other cities, too, the missionaries are able to work without resistance. In every church, Paul and Barnabas appoint *"elders"* (Acts 14:23)—men capable of being overseers of doctrine and discipline—and commit the new believers to their Lord.

Open Door for Gentiles

Paul and Barnabas retrace their steps through the highlands of Pisidia to coastal Pamphylia. They come to Perga, where the humid lowland had tested their health. Paul's health has improved, so they preach in Perga and then continue to Attalia. From there, they sail back to Syrian Antioch, where the missionary journey began. From start to finish, the trip covers about 1,500 miles. When they arrive in Antioch, they report to the congregation what God has done and how the door of faith has been opened for the Gentiles. God had sovereignly appointed Paul as an apostle to the Gentiles, and the predominantly Gentile church at Antioch is pleased with the results of the missionary effort. Paul and Barnabas remain in Antioch with the disciples *"no little time"* (14:28).

Personalize this lesson.

Paul and Barnabas kept going, whether accepted or persecuted. Paul and Barnabas did not take persecution as a sign that they should go home; they simply went to another place and began again. Nothing in Jesus' teaching or in the disciples' own lives had led them to believe that their efforts would be met with approval and acceptance.

Think about the ministry in which you are currently involved or which you hope to be part of in the future. What would "success" look like in that ministry? Offer up your ministry to God, and ask Him help you focus on what He desires from you in that work. As you pray, release to Him any measures of success that are different from His.

The Apostolic Council
Acts 15

❖ Acts 15:1-3—Paul and Barnabas Go to Jerusalem

1. What causes dissension in the Antioch church?

   _____

   _____

2. Why was resolving this controversy so important?

   _____

   _____

❖ Acts 15:4-11—Peter Defends the Gentiles' Faith at the Jerusalem Council

3. Some scholars believe at least two different meetings were held during this council. Read Acts 15:4-21 and Galatians 2:1-10. What was the basic content of each meeting?

   _____

   _____

   _____

4. Why do you think it was so important to establish the doctrine of salvation by faith alone? (See also Ephesians 2:8-9.)

   _____

   _____

   _____

5. How does Peter defend Gentile believers' faith?

    _____

    _____

6. How does Peter say a person is saved?

    _____

    _____

❖ Acts 15:12-21—James Offers Guidelines for Believers

7. Why do you think Paul and Barnabas present the accounts of the signs and wonders right after Peter's defense of the Gentiles?

    _____

    _____

8. What argument in verse 14 does James give for fully accepting Gentiles as "saved"?

    _____

    _____

9. James uses Amos 9:11-12 to support his argument. According to this Old Testament prophecy, how long has God been concerned with the Gentiles' salvation?

    _____

    _____

10. What leadership qualities do you see in James?

    _____

    _____

    _____

11. What can you learn from James about dealing with conflict?

    _____

    _____

    _____

12. What guidelines for the Gentiles does James suggest?

_____

_____

13. Read the following verses, and tell why you think James gives these specific guidelines?

    a.   1 Corinthians 6:18-20 _____

    _____

    b.   1 Thessalonians 4:3-8_____

    _____

❖ Acts 15:22-35—The Jerusalem Delegation Goes to Antioch

14. Who does the church send to Antioch along with Paul and Barnabus? What kind of men are they?

_____

_____

_____

15. Why might the Jerusalem church have chosen to send these particular men to Antioch?

_____

_____

_____

16. What examples of sensitivity do you see in the letter?

_____

_____

_____

17. How does the Antioch church respond to the letter?

_____

_____

❖ Acts 15:36-41—Paul and Barnabas Separate After a Disagreement

18. Why does Paul want to go on the second missionary journey?

_____

_____

19. What is the basis for the disagreement between Paul and Barnabas?

_____

_____

20. In what ways are both men right?

_____

_____

_____

21. In what ways are both men wrong?

_____

_____

_____

22. What are some positive and negative results of this separation?

_____

_____

_____

Apply what you have learned. The Jerusalem Council handled controversy with wisdom, respect, and love. Look back through the account in Acts 15 and find examples of how they showed love toward all the people involved in the conflict. Choose one of these principles and apply it in one of your relationships this week.

The Apostolic Council
Acts 15

The rapid growth of the Christian church brought serious problems typical of a growing church. The first crisis occurs when the news that Peter baptized Cornelius and other Gentiles in Caesarea reaches Jerusalem. Upon his return, Peter defends his actions so well that his brothers express gratitude to God for the Gentile conversions. A positive attitude toward missions is the result.

Now, Jewish believers from Jerusalem visit the Gentile Christians in Antioch and insist on circumcision for all Christians as a condition of salvation. Conflict erupts. The early church must decide whether all believers are bound by Mosaic regulations concerning circumcision and diet. Friction grows between Judaizers (legalistic Christians who still keep Jewish Law) and the growing number of newly baptized Gentile Christians, who are unsure about what former practices they must relinquish. Paul knows the issue could eventually split the church.

On to Jerusalem to Debate

Paul and Barnabas taught that salvation depends on faith in Jesus alone. To say salvation depends on faith in Christ plus something else (like circumcision) is to *"nullify the grace of God, for if righteousness were through the law, then Christ died for no purpose"* (Galatians 2:21). The discussions, in Antioch and later in Jerusalem, were no doubt heated. As Barnabas and Paul journey to Jerusalem in an attempt to resolve the matter, they tell churches along the way the stories of pagans coming to Christ. The churches rejoice because of the Gentile converts. The group causing trouble in Antioch does not represent the leadership of the church, for Paul and his companions receive a warm welcome in Jerusalem. All rejoice in what God has done through them. Many Pharisees have become Christians; some of them insist on circumcision for salvation. Paul, once a Pharisee, disagrees. He had not insisted that his associate Titus, a Greek, be circumcised (Galatians 2:3).

Scholars have debated the timing and sequence of the Jerusalem meetings for centuries. The writer of this Commentary supports the view that two sessions were held. Galatians 2:2 suggests Paul met to set an agenda and procedures with a smaller group, probably led by Peter, James, and others among the Twelve: *"I went up because of a revelation and set before them (though privately before those who seemed influential) the gospel that I proclaim among the Gentiles."* The subject for discussion seems to have been presented subsequently to a larger group.

Peter speaks first. He states that the Jerusalem church sent him on the mission that led him to the Gentiles, and that God declared the Gentiles clean and saved through faith in Christ alone. God gave the Gentiles the gift of the Holy Spirit, just as He had the first Jewish believers. Peter reasons that because the Law played no part in preparing Gentiles to receive a Savior, the Law should not be imposed on them now. Peter reminds his hearers that neither Jews nor Gentiles can do all that the Law requires. All need God's grace in Christ.

Then Barnabas and Paul give their testimonies. Instead of a lengthy review of their first missionary journey, they simply *"related what signs and wonders God had done through them among the Gentiles"* (15:12).

James Offers a Solution

James speaks last. James makes indisputable judgments—and his authority seems unquestioned. He recognizes that Gentiles are free from the Law, but two questions remain concerning the church's unity and purity. First, how can Jews brought up under Mosaic Law, for whom dietary restrictions have become a matter of conscience, live next to Gentiles and eat with them at the same table? Common meals were important to early Christianity. Second, does the Gentiles' freedom from the Law permit them to satisfy their sexual appetites and participate in pagan rites? These practical concerns also address the validity of being a people separated or *set apart* for God, a condition that began with God's covenant with Abraham.

James develops the following guidelines:

- ❖ Converted Gentiles should refrain from eating meat offered to idols and from taking part in pagan, sacrificial meals. The church must be as anti-idolatrous and anti-pagan as the synagogue.

❖ The church must maintain respect for women and avoid sexual license, religious or secular.

❖ Christians must not eat meat from strangled animals. (The Jews felt strongly about this matter.)

❖ Some cults drank blood during their rites. All Christians are to abstain from this practice.

The last two guidelines affect the unity and holiness of the church. James concludes by suggesting Gentile Christians observe these simple rules to avoid offending Jews.

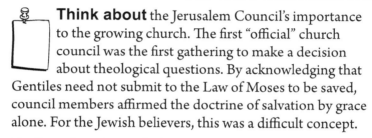

Think about the Jerusalem Council's importance to the growing church. The first "official" church council was the first gathering to make a decision about theological questions. By acknowledging that Gentiles need not submit to the Law of Moses to be saved, council members affirmed the doctrine of salvation by grace alone. For the Jewish believers, this was a difficult concept.

The Jerusalem Council's decision saved the church from being split into a Jewish church and a Gentile church. Believers today may not be divided on the issue of circumcision as an expression of faith, but some still treat other believers as inferior because they don't observe the same rites or have the same experiences. Romans 10:9 reminds us that *"if you confess with your mouth that Jesus is Lord and believe in your heart that God raised Him from the dead, you will be saved."* The New Testament assures us nothing else is necessary for salvation.

The Jerusalem Council deals successfully with the current issues confronting the church. Because the church in Antioch had sent a delegation to Jerusalem, Jerusalem returns the courtesy by sending Judas (also called Barsabbas) and Silas to Antioch. They take a letter containing the decision. The letter delights the church at Antioch, and the Jerusalem messengers comfort and strengthen the members.

Personalize this lesson.

The men from Judea, like many others throughout church history, wanted to add requirements for salvation beyond simple faith in Jesus. Wisely, the Jerusalem council ruled that faith is all that is necessary (though they did give some instructions for behavior). Take some time to reflect on the wonder of salvation by grace. What does it mean to you? Thank God that you do not have a burdensome list of rules to follow in order to know Him or receive eternal life. Worship God who offers salvation so freely, when it cost Him so much to give it.

On to Europe
Acts 16

Memorize God's Word: Romans 15:1-2.

❖ Acts 16:1-5—Paul and Silas Visit the Cities From Their First Missionary Journey

1. Why do you think Paul chooses Silas to go with him? (See Acts 15:22, 40.)

2. Describe Timothy's religious background (Acts 16:1-2; 2 Timothy 1:5; 3:14-15).

3. Why is Timothy circumcised?

4. Why do you think Paul did not require Titus to be circumcised (Galatians 2:1-3)?

❖ Acts 16:6-10—Paul Goes to Macedonia

5.   Read Proverbs 3:5-6. God clearly directed Paul not to go to Asia and Bithynia. What other plan does God have for Paul, and how does He make it known?

_____

_____

6.   How does Paul respond to this new direction?

_____

_____

7.   Observe the use of the personal pronoun *"we"* in this section of Acts. What new person is added to the missionary team at Troas?

_____

❖ Acts 16:11-15—Lydia Responds to the Gospel

8.   How does Paul begin to evangelize in Philippi?

_____

_____

9.   Why do you think he begins in this way? How might we follow this principle today?

_____

_____

10.   What two things enable Lydia to receive Paul's message?

_____

_____

❖ Acts 16:16-24—Paul and Silas Are Imprisoned in Philippi

11.   How does Paul respond to the slave girl's cries?

_____

_____

12. What is the power behind her behavior? Why does Paul respond to it in this way?

_____

_____

13. Why do the slave girl's owners take action against Paul and Silas?

_____

_____

14. What tactic do they use to get the rulers of Philippi to imprison Paul and Silas?

_____

_____

15. How would you describe Philippi's attitude toward the missionaries?

_____

_____

❖ Acts 16:25-40—Paul and Silas Are Released From Prison

16. What are Paul and Silas doing in prison before the earthquake? What do you think enables them to behave in this way?

_____

_____

17. How can God use the suffering in our lives to benefit us and others (16:25; 2 Corinthians 1:3-7)?

_____

_____

_____

18. What are the physical effects of the earthquake?

_____

_____

19. How does Paul tell the jailer he and his household can be saved?

_____

_____

20. What does the Philippian jailer do for Paul and Silas?

_____

_____

21. How does this behavior show an inward change in the Philippian jailer?

_____

_____

Apply what you have learned. Throughout Acts 16, we see Paul's sensitivity to the Holy Spirit's guidance. He received God's guidance in where to go, how to develop a successful strategy in Philippi, how to deal with enemy opposition, how to respond to suffering, and how to protect the believers he left behind.

Would you like to grow in your ability to listen to God? Make an appointment with a mature believer you respect and trust. Ask about how he or she learned to listen to God and be guided by the Holy Spirit. What attitudes are important? What Scriptures have been most helpful? Are there any pitfalls to avoid? Choose one truth that stands out to you from your time together, and begin to put it into practice.

On to Europe
Acts 16

Driven by the Holy Spirit and perhaps his own restless energy, Paul quickly decided that his missionary work must continue without Barnabas. He invited Silas to travel with him (Acts 15:40). As a Roman citizen, Silas had protection under the law, and his association with the Jerusalem Council would prove helpful in future dealings with the Judaizers.

Revisiting Cities From the First Journey

Starting from Antioch in Syria, Paul and Silas journey northwest to Tarsus, encouraging the churches in Syria and Cilicia. Turning northward at the Gulf of Issus, they follow a roundabout route west to Derbe, Lystra, and eventually Troas.

Luke records an event in Lystra that will have a significant impact on Paul's ministry. A young Christian, Timothy, joins Paul and Silas. His mother, Eunice, and grandmother are Jewish believers; his father is an unbelieving Greek. According to Mosaic Law, Eunice's marriage to a Gentile would be considered illegal and her children illegitimate. Because such children inherited their mother's nationality, Timothy is considered Jewish. However, because of his mixed parentage and the fact that he lives far away from the strict codes of Jerusalem, Timothy has not been circumcised as prescribed by Jewish Law. Knowing that the missionaries will meet many Jews familiar with Timothy's background, Paul circumcises him to avoid problems in his ministry. The friendship that develops between these two servants of God lasts the rest of Paul's life.

The Macedonian Call

Paul, Silas, and Timothy travel to Iconium, visiting churches founded on the first trip and delivering *"the decisions"* of the Jerusalem Council (16:4). The compromise permits Gentiles to join the church without circumcision or compliance with most other Mosaic restrictions.

Acts 16:6-10 presents a powerful picture of the Trinity. After Iconium, Paul seems to have several possible routes in mind that God blocks until they reach Troas. According to verse 6, *"the Holy Spirit"* keeps them from going south to Asia; according to verse 7, the *"Spirit of Jesus"* will not let them go north to Bithynia; and according to verse 10, through a vision of the man from Macedonia, God calls them to preach the gospel there. At this point, Luke begins to use the pronoun *we*, indicating that he has joined the group. He probably preaches with Paul as the four men take the gospel from Asia into Europe.

Lydia, Seller of Purple

The voyage from Troas to Macedonia takes two days. After landing at the port city of Neapolis, they go inland to Philippi, a Roman colony known as a military, economic, and political center during Paul's time. Paul wants to worship on the Sabbath but finds no synagogue in this city. On the edge of town near a river, he locates a small prayer group of God-fearing women. They welcome the missionaries, listen to their messages, and embrace their faith. One of the women is Lydia, a businesswoman who sells purple cloth and dye. Luke notes that the first convert in Europe is a woman. She and her household are baptized, probably in the river outside Philippi. Lydia immediately invites the four missionaries to make her home their headquarters while in Philippi, evidence of her gift of hospitality.

Think about Lydia's influence in Paul's ministry. She opened her home to Paul and those traveling with him. Her generosity may have prompted the offerings he later received from the Philippians. Paul's love for the Philippian church is evident in his affectionate letter to them: *"I thank my God in all my remembrance of you, always in every prayer of mine for you all making my prayer with joy, because of your partnership in the gospel from the first day until now"* (Philippians 1:3-5). How could you use your God-given gifts to build up others, as Lydia did? How could you partner with other believers in preaching the gospel?

Jailed With an Apology

One day as the missionaries go to their place of prayer, a slave girl with a divining spirit begins to follow them. She tells fortunes, for which her owners collect a fee. Because she constantly follows them, shouting they are *"servants of the Most High God"* (Acts 16:17), Paul becomes irritated. He orders the evil spirit to leave her, which it does. Even though the girl proclaims the truth, testimony from demons is not acceptable. Jesus did not permit demons to acknowledge Him, but cast them out. Having lost their source of income, the girl's owners become angry with Paul and Silas. They drag them before the rulers and accuse them of wrongful teaching. A mob attacks the missionaries, and the magistrates order them stripped, beaten, and jailed.

Despite their severe beatings and discomfort from the stocks, Paul and Silas pray and sing. At midnight, an earthquake rocks the prison, opening locked doors and unfastening the prisoners' chains. The jailer awakens. Assuming the prisoners have escaped and knowing he will be held responsible, he draws his sword to kill himself. Paul shouts that the prisoners are still there. The jailer then kneels before Paul and Silas and asks how to be saved. They answer, *"Believe in the Lord Jesus"* (Acts 16:31). After Paul and Silas share the gospel, the jailer and his household believe and are baptized. The jailer brings the men to his own house and feeds them.

When the magistrates learn that Paul and Silas are Roman citizens, they become frightened, realizing they have beaten and imprisoned Roman citizens without trial. They tell the jailer to let them go, but Paul refuses to leave quietly. He could have demanded justice but settles for a public apology, perhaps to make it easier for the new believers they will soon leave behind. Once freed, Paul, Silas, and Timothy visit Lydia and the young Christian community before departing. Luke apparently remains in Philippi to help the new church.

Personalize this lesson.

✓ When Paul traveled through Phrygia and Galatia, the Lord seemed to bring him to a halt. Paul responded by moving from Asia to Europe. Because he had the certainty of God's call to preach the gospel, he continued to seek the Lord's guidance for where and when to preach.

Spend some time in prayer over a ministry to which God has called you. (If you have a family, remember that they are part of your God-given ministry.) Recommit this ministry to God. Ask Him to confirm if you should continue in this ministry, or if He has something new for you. Seek His guidance in how to carry out your ministry—don't assume you should do it the way it has always been done. If you have not already done so, you may want to enlist a prayer partner for your ministry so that you can listen together for God's guidance. Commit to a regular time to seek God's guidance for your ministry.

In the Heartland of Greece
Acts 17

Memorize God's Word: Acts 17:30.

❖ Acts 17:1-9—Paul and Silas Evangelize Thessalonica

1. What does Paul do in the synagogue in Thessalonica?

   _____

   _____

2. Using Paul's example and 2 Timothy 2:15, explain what God's desire is for each Christian.

   _____

   _____

   _____

3. What steps do you think a Christian needs to take to be able to "[handle] *the word of truth*" accurately (2 Timothy 2:15)?

   _____

   _____

   _____

4. List the different responses in Thessalonica to Paul's teaching (17:4-5).

   _____

   _____

   _____

5. How is the Jews' complaint to city authorities against Paul and Silas actually a compliment?

_____

_____

6. What specific charge disturbs the authorities?

_____

_____

❖ Acts 17:10-15—Paul and Silas Move on to Berea

7. How does Luke describe the Jews of Berea, and why?

_____

_____

8. What effect do the Jews from Thessalonica have on Paul's work in Berea?

_____

_____

9. How do the Jews' actions affect the spread of the gospel? (See also Acts 17:1-9).

_____

_____

❖ Acts 17:16-21—Paul Goes to Athens Alone

10. What does Paul discover in Athens that _"provoked"_ (17:16) him? What does he do about the problem?

_____

_____

11. How would you describe the people of Athens, including their opinions of Paul?

_____

_____

❖ Acts 17:22-34—Paul Preaches to Athens' Leaders

12. Which truths about God does Paul include in his sermon?

_____

_____

13. What does Paul say about people?

_____

_____

14. Which truth in this sermon means the most to you, and why?

_____

_____

_____

15. What can you learn about sharing the gospel from Paul's example in Athens?

_____

_____

16. What are the results of Paul's visit to Athens?

_____

_____

❖ Selected Verses—The Nature and Results of Idolatry

17. Define *idolatry*, and describe some idols people "worship" today.

_____

_____

_____

18. What can you learn about idolatry or its consequences from the following verses?

   a.   Exodus 20:4 _____

_____

b.   Ezekiel 14:6-8 _____

_____

_____

c.   Galatians 5:19-21 _____

_____

_____

19. How can we avoid setting up "idols" in our lives today—things
that we put above God in our hearts, or that we look to to meet
our needs instead of Him?

_____

_____

_____

_____

Apply what you have learned. When Paul
addressed the Athenians, he used a different
approach from what he and other evangelists
usually used. Instead of using the Hebrew Scriptures—
which would have been foreign to his audience—he
used Greek literature and philosophy. His wisdom and
sensitivity as a cross-cultural minister gives us an example
we all can learn from. Who do you long to see come to
truth? Instead of using Scriptures that are foreign to them,
or telling them where they are wrong, learn from Paul.
What do you have in common with them that you could
build on? How can you affirm them and win their trust?
Ask God to give you wisdom and sensitivity as you talk
with unbelievers this week.

In the Heartland of Greece
Acts 17

Trouble in Thessalonica

After their experience in Philippi, Paul, Silas, and Timothy travel west 100 miles to Thessalonica. Once the capital of Macedonia, Thessalonica is prosperous because of its location on the Imperial Highway and its position as chief port for the northern inlets of the Aegean Sea. Exotic Eastern religions abound, as well as worship of the Roman emperor. Following his usual strategy, Paul begins his mission in the Jewish synagogue. For three weeks, he meets with a group on the Sabbath and explains, using the Old Testament prophecies, that Jesus is the Messiah, who was to suffer and rise from the dead. Only a few Jews believe, but many God-fearing Greeks and some well-respected women are converted. Women seem to have more freedom in Thessalonica than in other places.

The Jews, always a minority group in Thessalonica, become jealous when they see Paul making inroads into their group. Carefully planning their tactics and knowing that a small group can incite a crowd, they stir up trouble in the city. Because Paul is staying with Jason, the mob attacks Jason's house. Not finding Paul and Silas there, they drag Jason and other Christians to the magistrates. They accuse Jason of harboring criminals who are traveling around stirring up the people. The local officials, called *politarchs*, are upset, but after Jason and the others post bail, they release them. As a result of this incident, Paul's friends in Thessalonica smuggle Paul and Silas out of town at night. They head for Berea, 50 miles southwest.

> **Think about** the unbelieving Jews' complaint against Paul and Silas: *"These men who have turned the world upside down have come here also"* (Acts 17:6). Their preaching had changed lives. As new believers impacted the communities in which they lived, it seemed the world was turning upside down. Ask yourself, what can I do to impact my "world" or community?

The Noble Bereans

At the local synagogue in Berea, Paul and Silas find the Berean Jews willing to test the missionaries' teaching against the Scripture with hearts and minds open to the truth. They convert in large numbers, as do many Greek men and women.

But the Jews of Thessalonica are stubborn and determined, so they travel 50 miles to Berea to hinder Paul's ministry. In spite of the harassment, the church there flourishes because of the eagerness and interest of the people—many of high standing. Paul then moves 60 miles to Athens, leaving Silas and Timothy to complete the first stage of establishing a congregation in Berea. Later he will send for them. By this time he is keeping in touch with congregations in Philippi, Thessalonica, Berea, Athens, and Corinth, sending missionaries to them when possible and beginning to write letters to the various churches. He probably wrote 1 Thessalonians, his first epistle, during his stay in Corinth.

Paul Visits Athens

When Paul considered doing missionary work in Athens, he may have had mixed emotions. Athens had been the center of one of the world's great civilizations—rich in learning, art, and architecture—and the home of philosophers still read today. But in Paul's time, Alexandria had replaced Athens as the center of learning and culture. Tarsus had become its equal. Commercially, Corinth had become superior. But symbolically, Athens remained the center of the Hellenistic world.

A lively town, the center of Athens holds a huge marketplace called the agora. There, Athenians exchange news or listen to Stoic and Epicurean philosophers argue. The agora also serves as a "soapbox" for anyone with new ideas.

Paul arrives in Athens several days before any of his company and probably spends time getting acquainted with the city. Statues are everywhere, some dating from the golden age of Pericles (5th and 4th centuries BC). The people of Paul's day view the statues and monuments as embodying pagan gods. Such obvious idolatry offends Paul. As a rabbi, Paul preaches to the Jews and their adherents on the Sabbath; during the week, he debates in the marketplace. His presence creates much intellectual curiosity. To some he is just one more transient philosopher trying to gather an audience and be paid a fee. Luke reports several titles given to him, such as *"babbler"* and preacher of *"foreign divinities"* (17:18). Close by, on a high rocky ridge known as Mars Hill, is the Areopagus, where the city council meets. The Areopagus refers not just to a location but to the highest official body in Athens. When Paul is given the opportunity to address the city council, some of the philosophers escort him to the Areopagus.

Paul Lectures to the Areopagus

His message stirs great interest and continues to be studied and discussed by historians and theologians today. Paul begins his address in a complimentary way to gain the attention of his audience and to diminish their antagonism. He tries to establish a common bond by noting how religious they are and mentioning the altar inscribed to the unknown god. He points out that this God whom they have unknowingly honored is the One he is preaching about. He proclaims God as Creator and Ruler of the universe. Paul's statement that *"He [God] made from one man every nation of mankind"* (17:26) refers to Adam. For him and all who follow, God provided time, space, and a plan for their lives. In 17:27, Paul states that man's purpose on earth is to seek God. He then quotes their own poets. Acts 17:30 begins the thoroughly Christian part of Paul's message. Well aware of the Athenian accomplishments in philosophy, art, religion, and knowledge, Paul refers to their *"ignorance"* (17:30). God, he assures them, overlooks ignorance, but He has *"fixed a day"* (17:31) of judgment. Without naming Jesus, Paul says that the only way to escape that judgment is to repent and believe in *"the man whom [God] has appointed; of this He has given assurance to all by raising Him from the dead"* (17:31).

Paul gets a mixed reaction when he speaks of the *"resurrection of the dead"* (17:32). Some mock him. To those who believe in the theory of the soul's immortality without the concept of physical resurrection, Paul's sermon seems foolish and unreasonable. Some people, however, believe the message.

Personalize this lesson.

The Bereans had two very positive things going for them. They were eager and open to new teaching—but they checked it out against Scripture to make sure it was true. Many of us lack the balance the Bereans had. Either we are closed to new ideas, limiting our growth, or we accept new ideas too readily, without checking them out, leaving us vulnerable to spiritual error. Do you lean too far on one side or the other? Ask God to show you if you have closed yourself to anything new that He wants you to know. Ask Him also if you have too easily believed anything without checking it out. Respond to whatever He shows you.

The Gospel Comes to Corinth
Acts 18:1-17

Memorize God's Word: Acts 17:30.

❖ Acts 18:1-8—Paul Arrives in Corinth and Begins Ministry

1. Read 1 Corinthians 1:20-24 to discover what Paul is thinking as he begins his ministry in Corinth. What is his assessment of Greek wisdom and philosophy?

    _____

    _____

2. What is to be the sole focus of Paul's preaching in Corinth?

    _____

    _____

3. What new friends does Paul make in Corinth, and what are their common interests (18:1-3)?

    _____

    _____

4. What place do they have in his ministry (Romans 16:3-5)?

    _____

    _____

5. How would you describe Paul's work among the Jews in Corinth?

    _____

    _____

6. What is their response?

    _____

    _____

7. What is Paul's reaction to their opposition?

    _____

    _____

8. Paul explains his vision for this congregation in 1 Corinthians 12:12-26. What, according to Paul, are several ways we can contribute to unity in the body of Christ (1 Corinthians 12:12-14, 25-26)?

    _____

    _____

    _____

    _____

❖ Acts 18:9-17—Paul Remains Faithful Under Opposition

9. What do you learn about the character of God from this passage?

    _____

    _____

10. What do you learn about Paul?

    _____

    _____

11. What charges do the Jews bring against Paul in Gallio's court?

    _____

    _____

12. What happens after Gallio throws Paul's case out of court?

    _____

    _____

❖ Selections From 1 Thessalonians—A Heartfelt Letter

13. Read 1 Thessalonians 1:3-10. In what specific ways does Paul praise the Thessalonian believers?

_____

_____

_____

14. Read 1 Thessalonians 2:6-12, and list some ways Paul disciples these new Christians while in Thessalonica.

_____

_____

_____

15. What kind of report about the Thessalonian church did Timothy bring to Paul in Corinth (1 Thessalonians 3:2-10)?

_____

_____

16. What does Paul teach about what will happen to believers upon Jesus' return (1 Thessalonians 4:13-18)?

_____

_____

_____

17. What effect should believing the promise about Jesus' return have on believers?

_____

_____

_____

18. What does God provide for His people to ready them for Jesus' return (1 Thessalonians 5:23-24)?

_____

_____

❖ Selections From 2 Thessalonians—Jesus' Return for Unbelievers

19. What does Paul say will happen to unbelievers when Jesus returns (2 Thessalonians 1:5-10)?

_____

_____

20. Read 2 Thessalonians 2. Why were the Thessalonians confused about the teaching concerning Jesus' return (2:1-2)?

_____

_____

21. In 2 Thessalonians 2:13-16, how does Paul encourage the Christians in Thessalonica?

_____

_____

_____

Apply what you have learned. Reread Paul's description of his ministry to the Thessalonians in 1 Thessalonians 2:5-12. As you think about the opportunities you have to encourage and build up other believers, which of these principles most appeals to or challenges you? How could you put this principle into practice? Choose one action you could take to practice Paul's style of discipling, and put it into your schedule for the coming week.

The Gospel Comes to Corinth
Acts 18:1-17

An Unlikely Prospect

Why did God's Spirit abruptly lead Paul to Corinth after such a brief time in Athens (18:1)? A close examination of the Greek text suggests he may have been compelled to leave, but no warm welcome awaited him at his destination.

Corinth, which dates back to the 8th century BC, was a trade and commercial center less than 50 miles from Athens. The people of this cosmopolitan city were open to new ideas. Under Julius Caesar, Corinth had become a haven for many cultures: Roman, Greek, Eastern, and Jewish. Like most seaports, it had a high crime rate and many opportunities for immorality. The Greek historian Strabo wrote about a temple to Aphrodite there served by 1,000 prostitutes. So loose was the moral conduct that the Greeks had a phrase to *Corinthianize*, meaning to live an immoral life without restraint. Understanding this setting helps us to better comprehend the letters Paul wrote to the Corinthians—two of which survive as 1 and 2 Corinthians in the New Testament.

Paul's ministry in Corinth begins, as usual, with a visit to the synagogue. Then he moves out into the community, conversing, instructing, debating, and finally establishing a fellowship. He builds his case for the gospel on the experience of his hearers, using either selections from the Old Testament or references from pagan religions or philosophy. Then he progresses to the life and teachings of Jesus, the Crucifixion, and the Resurrection. He trains local leadership or leaves one of his associates in charge when he moves on. Whenever possible, Paul revisits the congregations and also writes letters to them. During his 18-month stay in Corinth, he writes letters to many of the established churches elsewhere. His first letter to the Thessalonians, probably written from

Corinth, is believed to be the oldest book in the New Testament. The second letter to the Thessalonians, Romans, and possibly Galatians also were written there.

Think about how Paul took a personal interest in the people he ministered to. He looked for a common interest: *"To the Jews I became as a Jew, in order to win Jews. ...To those outside the law I became as one outside the law… that I might win those outside the law….I have become all things to all people, that by all means I might save some"* (1 Corinthians 9:20-23). How important it is for us to be well-read and informed. Being careful to stay grounded in the Bible, we must be willing to learn how people think in our time and place, for we cannot isolate ourselves and expect to effectively communicate the gospel.

Among Paul's first friends and perhaps the first fruit of his ministry in Corinth is a Jewish couple, Aquila and Priscilla, who have come from Rome. Like Paul, they are tentmakers. He stays with them as he had with Lydia in Philippi and Jason in Thessalonica. By preaching in the synagogue and sharing the gospel with those he meets in the streets, he establishes a strong church in Corinth.

A Night Vision

Silas and Timothy come to Corinth, bringing good news and gifts from the Macedonians. The gifts allow Paul to give up manual labor for a time and devote his full energy to preaching. But the Jews oppose him for presenting Jesus as the long-awaited Messiah. Paul has given them an opportunity to hear the gospel; now he knows he is to turn to the Gentiles. By saying *"Your blood be on your own heads!"* (Acts 18:6), he indicates he has discharged his duty to his own people and will not be guilty of their damnation. However, even though he focuses his attention on the Gentiles, he stays in contact with the Jews. No longer able to preach in the synagogue, he preaches next door. His persistence is rewarded when Crispus (the leader of the synagogue) and his household confess faith in Jesus as Lord and are baptized by Paul. In the face of constant harassment from the Jews, Paul must have been discouraged, because God chooses to reassure him through a night vision. God tells Paul to keep witnessing and promises to be with him *"for* [He has] *many in this city who are My people"* (18:10).

Vindication From Rome

God uses a change in administration from Rome to encourage Paul when a new proconsul, Junius Annaeus Gallio, arrives. The Jews who oppose Paul hope to take advantage of Gallio's inexperience, and they haul Paul before the tribunal and accuse him of causing people to worship God unlawfully. Gallio senses a trap and refuses to hear the case. The frustrated Jewish community seizes Sosthenes, Crispus's successor as ruler of the synagogue, and beats him, but Gallio ignores the attack.

Letters to the Thessalonians

Paul lives in Corinth for some time after his court appearance and begins writing letters as part of his missionary effort. Earlier, he sent Timothy back to the Thessalonians from Athens. When Timothy returns to Corinth, his report distresses Paul. Paul writes to the Thessalonians expressing his concerns: Paul's opponents think he is not a true apostle, his motives are selfish, and he has no real love for Christians in Thessalonica.

In the first three chapters, Paul gives assurance that he loves them and is worthy of their love; and pagans were persecuting Christians there and urging them to return to sexual practices displeasing to God. Paul warns of the consequences of immoral behavior and encourages them to live lives that please God. His message in 1 Thessalonians is that Christ *will* return for believers. Although we cannot know the time, our hearts must be established in holiness before God and in love for one another. In 2 Thessalonians, he continues teaching about the Second Coming, emphasizing that believers must separate themselves from people who claim to be Christians yet live ungodly lives.

Personalize this lesson.

✓ It is easy to get the impression from Acts that Paul is fearless. After all, he continues to boldly preach the gospel despite receiving vicious beatings and repeated death threats. But in Acts 18:9-11, we see that Paul apparently does have fears. God does not condemn him for these fears, but promises to be with him and to protect him.

Do you have any fears connected with following Jesus and serving Him? Bring your fears before the Lord and ask Him to speak to you about them. Listen for His voice in prayer, as you read the Scriptures, and through any other means He might use to encourage you. Write down what you sense Him saying to you, and refer to these words when fears threaten to return.

The Third Journey Begins
Acts 18:18-28

❖ Acts 18:18—Paul Leaves Corinth

1. Compare Acts 18:11 with Acts 18:18. How long does Paul stay in Corinth?

   _____

   _____

2. What kind of people make up the church he establishes there? (See also 1 Corinthians 6:9-11; 12:2.)

   _____

   _____

   _____

3. According to 1 Corinthians 1:4-8, 30 and 6:11, what did God do for the Corinthians who turned to Christ?

   _____

   _____

4. What truths about God do you see from His ministry to the Corinthians?

   _____

   _____

   _____

❖ Acts 18:19-21—Paul Briefly Visits Ephesus

5.   What do you think Paul accomplishes in Ephesus during his brief stay?

_____

_____

6.   Read James 4:13-16 and Proverbs 16:9. How does Paul apply these principles to his potential return to Ephesus?

_____

_____

7.   How can you apply these truths to your own plans?

_____

_____

❖ Acts 18:22—Paul Returns to Antioch

8.   Name one or two cities that stand out to you on Paul's second missionary journey (Acts 15:39–18:22), and explain why you chose them.

_____

_____

_____

9.   From Galatians 2:11-13, describe an important and painful incident that occurs in Paul's home church in Antioch.

_____

_____

10. Read Galatians 2:14-16. What does Paul remind the Jewish Christians?

_____

_____

_____

11. Do you think it is easy to slip away from this truth today? If so, why?

_____

_____

12. God uses Paul to bring about His discipline in Peter's life. Read Hebrews 12:5-11. What motivations are behind God's discipline of believers?

_____

_____

_____

❖ Acts 18:23-28—Paul Begins a Third Journey; Apollos Preaches in Ephesus

13. What is the purpose of Paul's third journey?

_____

_____

14. How would you describe Apollos?

_____

_____

15. Read Matthew 3:1-6 and Luke 3:3-4, referring to the *"baptism of John"* (Acts 18:25). What truths about Jesus would Apollos have been teaching?

_____

_____

_____

16. Priscilla and Aquila see gaps in Apollos's knowledge of Jesus. They invite him to their home and explain more about God and His way. What does their meeting with Apollos accomplish?

_____

_____

❖ Selections From Galatians—A Letter to the Galatian Church

17. Read Galatians 1:6-9. Why is Paul upset with the Galatian church?

_____

_____

18. How does Paul defend his authority as an apostle presenting the gospel of grace (Galatians 1:11-16)?

_____

_____

19. Review Galatians 2:16. How would you summarize Paul's teaching about how a person is saved? (See also Galatians 3:10-14, 22.)

_____

_____

20. Read Galatians 5:1-4, 13. What facts about freedom in Christ does Paul give here?

_____

_____

Apply what you have learned. When Priscilla and Aquila heard Apollos's teaching, they could easily have criticized him or avoided him. Instead, they took him aside and *"explained to him the way of God more accurately"* (Acts 18:26). As a result, he embraced the truth and became a powerful minister of God.

Make a list of the attitudes and actions you think Priscilla and Aquila may have needed to approach Apollos in this way. Which one would you most like to emulate? Write down the first step you could take to grow in this area so that you will be prepared to graciously share truth with fellow believers who are in error.

The Third Journey Begins
Acts 18:18-28

On the Move

As Paul ministers in Corinth, he thinks of the converts in other cities such as Philippi, Iconium, and Lystra where he founded congregations. Then there is Ephesus, still to be won for his Master. Suddenly he is moved with a compelling desire to return to home base, share his experiences, receive encouragement, and have fellowship with those who originally sent him on missionary journeys, making him willing to undertake the difficult trip of over 1,000 miles by sailing vessel.

Leaving Corinth must have been hard for Paul, because he had spent enough time there to build strong friendships. He does, however, take Priscilla and Aquila with him. Throughout the remainder of Luke's account, Priscilla's name comes first, hinting that she had spiritual gifts that put her in an important leadership role in the early church. However, in a letter mentioning a house church that met in the couples' home, Paul refers to Aquila first as the head of the household.

While visiting a Christian congregation in Cenchreae, a port on the Aegean Sea, Paul cuts off his hair, indicating his fulfillment of a Nazirite vow, a common custom in Old Testament times (Numbers 6:5). Perhaps the difficulties in Corinth caused him to seek strength by making such a vow, or perhaps he was giving thanks for God's protection. Luke may have included this incident to show that as a Christian, Paul still observed some Jewish practices.

Luke states briefly, *"They came to Ephesus"* (Acts 18:19). The sailing distance of about 300 miles between Cenchreae and Ephesus gives Paul, Priscilla, and Aquila time to discuss all that occurred in Corinth and to plan for the evangelization of Ephesus. Paul stays in Ephesus only a short time. Members of the synagogue there request that he stay longer, but he declines, saying that if God so wills, he will return. Then he sets sail, leaving Priscilla and Aquila in Ephesus.

On Paul's arrival in Caesarea, *"he went up and greeted the church"* (18:22), which may refer to a short detour to Jerusalem rather than to any congregation in Caesarea. Going on, Paul returns to Antioch in Syria, the mother church of all missions to the Gentiles. He probably plans to spend the winter there because a sea journey back to Ephesus would be hazardous at that time. In Antioch, a conflict arises. Although Luke doesn't mention it, Paul refers to it in his letter to the Galatians, possibly written a year later. Peter has suddenly withdrawn from contact with Gentiles when men of the circumcision party—who teach that circumcision is necessary for salvation—arrive from Jerusalem. The other Jewish believers follow his lead. Paul confronts his hypocrisy *"before them all"* (Galatians 2:11-14).

Think about Paul's defense of the truth of the gospel. Keeping the Law to gain salvation was an issue that had to be resolved, not only for the sake of the church, but also for the good of Peter and the Jewish Christians. Paul was not saying the Law was not good, but that it had been fulfilled in Jesus Christ. Followers of Christ do not live according to the old Law, which regulated behavior, but according to the Spirit, who inspires and empowers believers' godly behavior.

After a time, Paul leaves Antioch, never to return. Rather than sail, he goes overland in a northwesterly direction through Cilicia and the Taurus Mountains to visit churches he established earlier. Paul's exact route is not known, but he finally reaches Ephesus, his base for at least the next three years.

Apollos in Ephesus

While Paul is making his final visit in Antioch and other regions, Apollos comes to Ephesus. Apollos was a Jew with a Greek name from Alexandria, Egypt. Alexandria was the foremost educational center, with a world-famous library. Apollos's knowledge of the Old Testament and his oratorical skill are impressive. He comes to Ephesus with a burning zeal to proclaim the gospel as he understands it.

Priscilla and Aquila are impressed by Apollos's message, but they realize he lacks knowledge of the living Lord Jesus. He seems to understand the implications of the Messianic references to Jesus in Old Testament prophecy, but his knowledge of baptism is limited to the baptism of repentance—that of John the Baptist. He does not realize that the Holy Spirit comes to baptize every believer into Christ, thereby indwelling the believer, sealing the believer for all eternity as God's possession, and empowering the believer for a fruitful life. Priscilla and Aquila teach him what he lacks in knowledge, and this brilliant man humbly accepts their teaching. When the day comes for him to launch out on his own, the church leaders at Ephesus send him to Corinth.

Missionary to the Galatians

Paul probably wrote his letter to the Galatians from Corinth. Part of it was in his handwriting, but most was dictated to a secretary. Galatians is divided into three parts: The first is autobiographical—Paul defends his apostleship, stressing that his authority comes directly from God. The second develops the theme of Galatians: People are not justified by the Law but through faith in Christ. Galatians is the only letter in which Paul does not express appreciation for his readers. Instead he calls them *"foolish Galatians!"* (Galatians 3:1). Paul was horrified to learn they were trying to please God by keeping the Law. The third part, chapters 5 and 6, deals with how believers are to live. Paul uses the term *"in Christ"* 43 times to describe the relationship between faith and the Christian life. He is determined that his new converts will not live in the bondage of legalism but will experience the freedom of the gospel of grace. To Paul, perhaps more than to any other writer of Scripture, we owe our understanding of the good news of justification by faith alone.

Personalize this lesson.

✓ Like the Christians in Galatia, we, too can fall into the trap of religiously thinking that we must perform to please God. But Paul says that the Christian life isn't about performing externals— it's about living by the Spirit (Galatians 3:2-4). A life pleasing to God comes by believing Him and responding to His Spirit's work in you.

What areas of your life are motivated by faith in God and the power of the Holy Spirit? What areas are motivated by duty, guilt, or keeping up appearances? What do the lists you just created reveal about you? Do you want to confess anything to God? Thank Him? Ask for help? This week, whether at work, home, church, or in the community, consciously trust in God to lead, motivate, and empower you in whatever you do.

Ministry in Ephesus
Acts 19:1-20

❖ **Acts 19:1-7—Paul Begins His Third Missionary Journey**

   1. Based on Acts 18:24-26 and 19:1-7, who had been teaching the disciples in Ephesus?

     _____

     _____

   2. What had been taught at this point about the Holy Spirit?

     _____

     _____

   3. What do the Ephesians do to prove they believe in Jesus?

     _____

     _____

   4. How does God verify their faith in Jesus?

     _____

     _____

❖ **Acts 19:8-10—Paul Teaches in Ephesus**

   5. Write several words or phrases that describe

     a. Paul's activity in Ephesus. _____

     _____

     _____

b. the Jews' response. _____

_____

_____

6. What are the results for those Jews, and for other Jews and
    Greeks in Asia?

_____

_____

7. How did God use the opposition in Ephesus for good?

_____

_____

8. How does Paul's example in Ephesus illustrate Jesus' teaching in
    John 12:24-25?

_____

_____

❖ Acts 19:11-16—Miracles Surround Paul's Ministry in Ephesus

9. How would you describe the city of Ephesus in Paul's day
    (19:23-28)?

_____

_____

10. Who is responsible for the miracles occurring during Paul's stay
    in Ephesus, and what one word does the Bible use to describe
    the miracles?

_____

_____

11. What aspects of God's character do you see in the way He
    reveals Himself in Ephesus?

_____

_____

12. What do you learn from the incident recorded here about the danger of trying to confront demonic activity without the God-given authority to use Jesus Christ's powerful name?

_____

_____

❖ Acts 19:17-20—Confessing and Abandoning Magic Arts

13. What happens in Ephesus after the Jewish exorcists are exposed as impostors (19:17)?

_____

_____

14. Read Deuteronomy 18:9-14. Which of the practices listed there are still practiced in your culture today? (Use a dictionary to help you understand these practices, if necessary.)

_____

_____

_____

_____

_____

15. How does God feel about the practices you listed in question 14?

_____

_____

_____

16. What do the Ephesians do to separate themselves from their former practices?

_____

_____

17. *For personal thought:* Is there anything you have dabbled with that displeases God and puts you at spiritual risk? If so, how might you separate yourself from it?

_____

_____

_____

_____

_____

_____

Apply what you have learned. Paul preached the gospel to both Jews and Gentiles by *"reasoning and persuading"* (Acts 19:8-9). Are you prepared to make intellectual arguments for your faith? If not, go to your church library, Christian bookstore, or online source to research reasons for believing in Jesus and ways to respond to common objections. Make a plan for when you will read it.

Ministry in Ephesus
Acts 19:1-20

Corinth and Ephesus were twin cities separated by the Aegean Sea, an arm of the Mediterranean. Ephesus, located in Asia, and Corinth, in Europe, were seaport towns with the social and moral deficits common to great commercial centers of that day. As centers of trade, they served as vantage points from which Paul could oversee his missionary enterprises. He spent more time in these two cities than in any others during his ministry.

When Paul first attempted to go to Ephesus, the Holy Spirit led him to change his plans, and he ended up in Troas. The second time, he stayed only briefly in Ephesus while on his way to Jerusalem and Antioch, but he left Priscilla and Aquila there to lay the foundations of his work. On his third visit, Paul established his base for ministry.

Paul's First Encounter in Ephesus

When Paul arrives in Ephesus, he immediately finds some disciples who have never heard of the Holy Spirit. Some Bible scholars think these Ephesians belonged to a group of followers of John the Baptist. However, the text implies they were disciples of Jesus. Another explanation is that Apollos had taught them before he met Priscilla and Aquila.

Paul questions the disciples: *"Did you receive the Holy Spirit when you believed?"* (Acts 19:2). He finds they have never heard of the Holy Spirit. He explains that John's preparatory baptism is no longer sufficient. They accept baptism in the name of Jesus, confessing Him as Lord. Paul lays his hands on them. The Holy Spirit comes upon the believers and they experience two signs: speaking in tongues and prophesying.

The practice of laying on hands appears on a variety of occasions in Acts. Sometimes people received the Holy Spirit through the laying on of hands (8:17; 9:17; 19:6). Other times the Holy Spirit came without laying on hands (2:4; 4:31; 10:44; 11:15). The laying on of hands was also connected with other forms of spiritual ministry such as conferring spiritual blessing, healing, commissioning to a particular task or ministry, or imparting gifts of the Spirit.

From Synagogue to Lecture Hall

Many times Paul was tempted to give up on the Jews because of their resistance to the gospel, yet he always returned to them. He encountered trouble in almost every synagogue in Asia Minor, but he loved his people and felt that their heritage prepared them to believe and receive the good news of Christ. So in Ephesus, as in other cities, he begins his missionary efforts in the synagogue, centering his messages on the arrival of God's kingdom, pointing out to the Jews that their ancient hope is fulfilled in Jesus' life, death, and resurrection. But for many the Cross is still a stumbling block. While Paul emphasizes the lordship of Jesus and the outpouring of the Holy Spirit, the Jews believed the Crucifixion was the curse God placed on Jesus because He claimed to be God.

Acts 19:9 describes the reactions of those who refuse to accept the gospel. Many translations use the word *stubborn*; the King James Version describes their attitude as *"hardened."* The letter to the Hebrews warns Jewish believers not to miss what God is saying because of the same attitude: *"Today, if you hear His voice, do not harden your hearts"* (Hebrews 3:7-8). After three months, Paul leaves the synagogue.

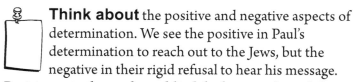

Think about the positive and negative aspects of determination. We see the positive in Paul's determination to reach out to the Jews, but the negative in their rigid refusal to hear his message. Resistance to the truth can blind the heart and mind. It can lead to eternal death for an unbeliever and cause spiritual stagnation and a powerless life for a Christian. Believers who resist God wander in a spiritual wilderness, missing the blessing of fellowship with Jesus. But God is ready to forgive and restore.

The Kingdom, Power, and Glory

Paul and his disciples move their activities to the hall of Tyrannus, where Paul teaches daily for two years. The great miracles he performs attract the attention of the whole city, including some Jewish men who earn their living by casting out demons. After Paul comes to Ephesus, these men try to exercise power over demons by using Jesus' name. As we have seen before, demons can speak through the mouths of the people they possess. As the sons of Sceva try to use the power of Jesus' name, the demon who possesses the man being exorcised becomes angry because his authority is being threatened. He questions their right to use Jesus' name, and attacks, strips, and wounds the exorcists, who flee in defeat. The power of Jesus Christ overcomes the power of Satan through Paul's ministry, but that power is not meant to be used like a magic spell. Believers in Ephesus who had been practicing magic see this, confess their sins, burn their sorcery books, and surrender their lives to God. The result in Ephesus: *"the word of the Lord continued to increase and prevail mightily"* (19:20).

Think about the disastrous result of tampering with spiritual power. The occult is a realm of darkness. If we search for special knowledge through horoscopes, Ouiji boards, fortune tellers and the like, we are in danger of tapping into demonic forces. Read Deuteronomy 18:9-14 to see if any forbidden activities on God's list are a part of your life.

Personalize this lesson.

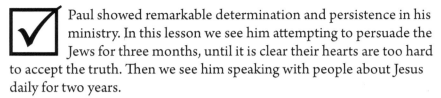 Paul showed remarkable determination and persistence in his ministry. In this lesson we see him attempting to persuade the Jews for three months, until it is clear their hearts are too hard to accept the truth. Then we see him speaking with people about Jesus daily for two years.

What does God want you to learn from Paul about determination and persistence? Spend time in prayer, asking God if there is any assignment or relationship from Him that you are tempted to give up on too early. Ask Him to strengthen you to continue with the ministry to which He has called you despite difficulty, discouragement, or even opposition.

Lesson 21

The Ephesian Riot
Acts 19:21-41

Memorize God's Word: Romans 1:16.

❖ **Acts 19:21-27—Demetrius Opposes Paul's Teachings**

1. How does Paul decide to go to Jerusalem (19:21; 20:22)? What do you think this means?

2. What future plans reveal Paul's missionary zeal?

3. Which two trades in Ephesus are threatened by so many Ephesians following *"the Way"* (19:23)? (See also Acts 19:17-20.)

4. Who is the real mastermind behind Demetrius's opposition, and what are his tactics, according to the following verses?

   a. John 8:44 _____

   b. 1 Peter 5:8_____

5.   In 1 Corinthians 15:32, how does Paul describe enemies like Demetrius and his attackers?

_____

_____

6.   How might the following verses comfort and encourage Christians being attacked for their faith?

   a.   Psalm 91:14-16_____

_____

   b.   Romans 8:36-39_____

_____

   c.   1 John 4:4 _____

_____

❖ Acts 19:28-41—Ephesus in an Uproar

7.   What truths about human nature do you see in the account of the riot?

_____

_____

_____

_____

8.   The town clerk is in a position of power much like the mayor of a city today. What logic does he use to disperse the crowd?

_____

_____

9.   Why does he intervene?

_____

_____

In preparation for his visit to Rome, and with the events in Ephesus still fresh in his mind, Paul writes a letter to the Romans. The next two sets of questions will introduce you to some of the book's important doctrines.

❖ Selections From Romans—Man's Sinful Condition and God's Remedy

10. Read Romans 1:16-17. Why does Paul say he is not ashamed of the gospel?

    _____

    _____

11. When Paul writes Romans 1:18-32 describing God's wrath toward the pagan world, he may have had Ephesus in mind. From Romans 1:18-23, list several attitudes resulting in God's anger.

    _____

    _____

12. How do Paul's opponents in Acts 19:23-41 display these attitudes?

    _____

    _____

13. Romans 2:1-16 deals with moral (even religious) persons who live independently of Christ. How will God judge such persons?

    _____

    _____

14. Read Romans 3:21-23. How has God has provided the way for man to escape the judgment resulting from sin?

    _____

    _____

❖ Selections From Romans—Appropriating the Power of Salvation

15. Why does Paul find it impossible to obey God in his own strength (Romans 7:14-25)?

    _____

    _____

    _____

16. How has God made it possible for us to be holy (8:1-4)?

_____

_____

17. What resources does God make available to us to live the Christian life successfully (8:26-34)?

_____

_____

_____

18. Romans 12:1-2 sums up the commands Paul gives in Romans for living the Christian life. What do you think it means to *"present your bodies as a living sacrifice"* to God?

_____

_____

_____

Apply what you have learned. Although Paul regularly followed the Holy Spirit's leading, during the riot in Ephesus he nearly made an unwise and dangerous choice. The other disciples, and even some unbelieving friends, kept him away from the mob at the theater. God often speaks to us and warns us of danger through the counsel of others.

Do you have trusted advisers whom you can go to in a crisis, or when you face difficult decisions? Write down the names of three people who could give you wise input on challenging situations you might face. Choose mature, godly people who know you, know the Scriptures, and listen to God. If you need help or encouragement right now, make an appointment with one of them this week.

The Ephesian Riot
Acts 19:21-41

Luke shows Paul as a highly motivated person, always open to the Holy Spirit's leading, sometimes so forcefully led that he feels "driven." Under such drive, he has been laboring in Ephesus, the capital of Asia Minor. While there, Paul feels prompted to go to Jerusalem and then to Rome, the heart of the Empire.

Preparations

Paul devises a plan to bring believers with Jewish backgrounds and Gentile converts together: Hearing that the Jerusalem church is in constant financial need, he decides to visit some of his more prosperous Gentile missions, collect contributions from them, and personally take the money to Jerusalem. In preparation, he sends two of his helpers to Macedonia: Timothy (who later rejoins Paul in Corinth) and Erastus. Meanwhile, Paul stays in Ephesus.

When Religion Hurts Business

Demetrius and his friends in Ephesus are silversmiths who make images of the Greek goddess Artemis (or Diana, as the Romans called her). Apparently, enough people have become Christians that sales of the silver shrines of Artemis have dropped sharply, hurting the silversmiths' trade. Demetrius organizes a public protest. Although the real problem is loss of business, Demetrius appeals to the religious and civic emotions of the Ephesians. He testifies that Paul said a manmade god is no god at all, and because Paul has won people to Christ *"not only in Ephesus but in almost all of Asia"* (Acts 19:26), his teaching could lead to the destruction of Artemis and her temple—one of the seven wonders of the ancient world.

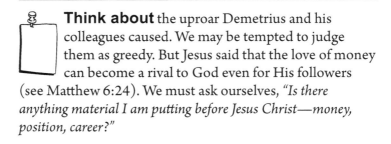

Think about the uproar Demetrius and his colleagues caused. We may be tempted to judge them as greedy. But Jesus said that the love of money can become a rival to God even for His followers (see Matthew 6:24). We must ask ourselves, *"Is there anything material I am putting before Jesus Christ—money, position, career?"*

Great Is Artemis of the Ephesians

Demetrius and other tradesmen stir up the people into a nasty mob and lead them to the huge amphitheater. The crowd is so confused, most of the people do not even know why they are there. When they hear of the potential threat to their local deity, Artemis, they begin shouting, *"Great is Artemis of the Ephesians!"* (19:34). Paul wants to confront the people, but his disciples fear for his life and hold him back. Some officials of the province send a message begging Paul not to enter the theater. When a local Jew named Alexander tries to speak to the mob, the people shout him down, yelling for two hours straight.

The End of the Matter

The town clerk finally quiets the mob. He argues that Paul and the Christians have not blasphemed Artemis and tells the people to make their complaints in court. He reminds the crowd that Ephesus is subject to the Romans, who could mistake their noisy gathering as a riot and invoke severe penalties. He then sends the crowd home.

Paul holds a final meeting with the disciples in Ephesus, travels around Greece for a while encouraging Christians there, and then goes back to Corinth to spend the winter. During the three months he spends in Corinth prior to visiting Jerusalem, Paul writes his masterpiece—a letter to the Romans.

The Gospel According to Paul

Paul writes the believers in Rome a formal letter—a theological presentation—in preparation for his stay there. This letter differs from most of Paul's letters, which were written quickly in response to some urgent question or situation. The Book of Romans is a thoughtfully written document. Aware that his preaching on Christianity with its emphasis on faith and God's grace is unacceptable in many areas, Paul feels it necessary to set forth a full explanation of the gospel as he understands it. He carefully organizes an argument for the faith in order to establish his credibility to the Christians in Rome.

Paul writes to a church he did not found and had never even visited. But he had long wanted to visit this congregation (Romans 15:23). No doubt Priscilla and Aquila had talked to him about the church in Rome, telling him of its problems and potential. Paul probably saw Rome as an ideal missionary center for the western part of the Roman Empire.

When Paul writes his letter to the Romans, Christian churches are no longer predominantly Jewish. Paul knows tension exists between Jewish and Gentile Christians; he may expect the same to be true in Rome. Some scholars feel that his letter to the Romans represents a final attempt at reconciling the two groups. Remember also, Paul wants to raise financial support for the church in Jerusalem; he relies on Jewish and Gentile believers in Rome to support his fundraising (see Romans 15:25-29), while at the same time hoping to use the project to bring the differing groups together.

Paul's presentation of the gospel in the book of Romans has become authoritative for all time. The letter continues to be helpful, especially when misguided leaders try to direct the church back into the bondage of legalism.

Romans has probably had more influence on the development of the Christian church than any of the other 12 New Testament books attributed to Paul. Reformer and theologian John Calvin wrote, "If a man has reached a true understanding of [Romans], he has a door of approach opened for him to the rarest treasures of Scripture." Martin Luther, in his *Translation of the New Testament*, notes, "The Epistle to the Romans is the chief book of the New Testament and purest Gospel." John Knox states, "It is the principal source book for the study of Paul's Gospel."

Personalize this lesson.

Paul's appeal in Romans 12:1-2 describes the path to growing spiritually and discovering God's will. Read these verses slowly and carefully. Think about what each phrase means, and what it would look like for you to apply it to your life. You may want to rewrite the passage in your own words. Prayerfully reflect on what God is saying to you through these verses and what He most wants you to take away from them right now.

A Long Way to Rome
Acts 20

Memorize God's Word: Acts 20:24.

❖ Acts 20:1-6—Paul Leaves Ephesus and Spends Three Months in Greece

1. Read 2 Corinthians 1:8-11. What emotions might Paul have experienced during the riot in Ephesus?

   _____

   _____

2. From verses 9-10, what does Paul choose, and what are the results?

   _____

   _____

   _____

3. With this in mind, read Acts 20:1. What might Paul have included in his farewell to the Ephesians?

   _____

   _____

4. What does Paul do on his way to Macedonia? What does it tell you about his walk with God?

   _____

   _____

   _____

❖ Acts 20:7-12—Paul Ministers in Troas on His Way to Jerusalem

5. What miracle occurs on Paul's last night in Troas?

    _____

6. What is the result of this miracle?

    _____

    _____

7. How would you describe Paul's ministry in Troas?

    _____

    _____

    _____

❖ Acts 20:13-24—Paul Begins His Farewell to the Ephesian Elders

8. What principles of personal ministry do you see in verses 17-21?

    _____

    _____

    _____

9. What do you learn about Paul's ministry of discipleship from the following verses?

    a. Philippians 4:9 _____

        _____

    b. 1 Thessalonians 2:8_____

        _____

10. Paul states that he served the Lord with *"all humility"* (20:19). What do you think this means?

    _____

    _____

    _____

11. Despite the difficulties, what other aspects of Paul's ministry do you learn of in verses 17-35?

_____

_____

_____

12. Read verses 22-24. In your own words, how do you think Paul feels as he thinks of going to Jerusalem?

_____

_____

_____

13. What do the following verses say about suffering because of a person's commitment to Christ?

a. 2 Timothy 3:12_____

_____

b. 1 Peter 4:12-14_____

_____

_____

❖ Acts 20:25-32—Paul Warns the Ephesian Elders About False Teaching

14. Compare Ezekiel 3:16-21 with Acts 20:25-27, and explain why Paul can say he is *"innocent of the blood of all"* (Acts 20:26).

_____

_____

_____

_____

15. How does this make it easier for Paul to leave the Ephesians, whom he loves so deeply?

_____

_____

16. What does Paul warn the Ephesian elders about? What is the origin of this opposition to truth?

_____

_____

❖ Acts 20:32-38—Paul and the Ephesian Elders Say Goodbye

17. To whom and to what does Paul entrust the Ephesians?

_____

_____

18. What two things can the *"word of* [God's] *grace"* (20:32) do for the Ephesians? What do you think each one means?

_____

_____

19. Has the study of the book of Acts helped you to do these two things? If so, how?

_____

_____

20. How do the Ephesians and Paul minister to each other as they say goodbye (20:36-38)?

_____

_____

Apply what you have learned. Have you said goodbye to someone you love? Maybe a close friend has moved, or a child is about to go off to college. Think about how you could commit this person to *"God and the Word of His grace."* What would that look like? How would it shape your prayers? Do you want to bless this person by letting him or her know you are trusting God to care for them?

A Long Way to Rome
Acts 20

Paul's time in Ephesus is blessed in spite of the opposition he encounters. Yet he decides to leave, resolving to pass through Macedonia and Achaia on his way to Jerusalem. He says, *"After I have been there, I must also see Rome"* (19:21). He leaves almost immediately after the riot in Ephesus, taking time to say good-bye to his disciples. Luke documents Paul's circuitous, turbulent journey to Rome.

Farewell to Macedonia

Certain that God is leading him to Rome, Paul makes plans for what he feels will be his final visit to the congregations he has established. He meets with local leaders, encouraging those who will be responsible for continuing his ministry in Ephesus. Paul goes directly to Macedonia. Paul's struggles with the Corinthian church are not discussed, although other texts say that Paul sent Titus from Ephesus to Corinth to deal with its problems. During his trip through Macedonia, Paul endures *"fighting without and fear within"* (2 Corinthians 7:5). Along the way, he receives word from Titus that the difficulty with the Corinthians has been resolved.

Paul plans to go to Corinth on the way to Jerusalem. After traveling through Macedonia, where his ministry is productive, he reluctantly stops in Greece for the winter. During his three-month stay in Corinth, Paul writes his letter to the Romans. After Corinth, Paul plans to sail directly to Syria so he can reach Jerusalem in time for Passover. But before he boards the boat, he learns of a plot to kill him during the voyage and wisely changes his plans, retracing his steps by land into Macedonia. Because the land route takes longer than a sea journey, he will not reach Jerusalem in time for Passover, but hopes to be there by Pentecost.

Seven men travel with Paul, possibly representing the congregations sending aid to the Christians at Jerusalem, which may be why Luke includes their places of origin. Two of them are not mentioned anywhere else in Scripture: Sopater and Secundus. Aristarchus, also involved in the riot at Ephesus, later accompanies Paul to Rome. Gaius is from Derbe, distinguishing him from the man by the same name who was dragged before the Ephesian mob. Timothy joins Paul at Lystra. Tychicus delivers Paul's letters to the Ephesians (Ephesians 6:21) and the Colossians (Colossians 4:7). Trophimus later causes Paul's arrest in Jerusalem. In 2 Corinthians 7:13, Paul indicates that Titus joins the group in Macedonia. All these companions go to Troas, but Paul stays in Philippi to observe Passover. The *"we"* references appear again, indicating that Luke joins Paul in Philippi.

Think about Paul's life. By building close relationships with people, he trained them to evangelize, establish, and nurture new churches. He not only taught them but traveled, worked, and lived with them, modeling a Christ-centered lifestyle. Most important, he built on the only real foundation—Jesus Christ—rather than on his own personality. As we work for God, how can we challenge and encourage others as Paul did?

A Farewell Supper in Troas

Paul, Luke, and the other visiting missionaries join the local believers at Troas, where Paul had received the Macedonian call. They meet to *"break bread"* (Acts 20:7). Although breaking bread often refers to the Eucharist, or Holy Communion, the term could also refer to the act of sprinkling salt on a loaf, reciting a blessing to God as Creator, breaking the bread, and distributing it to the group. Or, it could mean simply sharing a meal.

The meeting is held in an upper room reminiscent of the one in which the Lord ate the last supper with His disciples. Illuminated by oil lamps or candles, which burn a lot of oxygen, the room is stuffy. While Paul preaches, a young man named Eutychus sits on the sill of an open window, nods off to sleep, falls three floors to the ground, and dies. Paul goes downstairs, throws himself on the boy, and wraps his arms around him, restoring him to life in a manner similar to the Old Testament accounts of Elijah (1 Kings 17:21-22) and Elisha (2 Kings 4:32-36). Paul reassures the young man's friends that Eutychus is alive. They all go back upstairs and Paul resumes ministering to them until daybreak.

Farewell to the Ephesian Elders

After the meeting in the upstairs room in Troas, Luke and the missionaries sail for Assos. Paul decides to go alone by land through Mysia to Assos. At Assos, Paul boards the ship with Luke, and they continue to Mitylene. A year has passed since Paul left Ephesus. He is anxious to arrive in Jerusalem by Pentecost, but he wants to see the Ephesian elders, so he sends a message asking them to meet him at Miletus. That meeting produces Paul's only speech to a Christian audience in Acts. Luke undoubtedly takes careful notes as Paul speaks. Paul's emotional farewell message reveals his deep feelings for them.

His address contains three main themes: First, he talks about his ministry among the Ephesians. In verses 19 and 31, he says that he served the Lord with humility and tears. In verses 20, 25, and 27, he describes his ministry as declaring to them the *"whole counsel of God"* (20:27)—preaching against sin and declaring God's love through forgiveness. Second, he acknowledges that none of them *"will see* [his] *face again"* (20:25). It was to be their final parting in this life. Third, he instructs the elders of Ephesus about their responsibilities as leaders of the church. Paul challenges them to be *"overseers, to care for the church of God"* (20:28), warning that *"fierce wolves"* (20:29) will enter the flock, seeking to harm them and lead them astray.

After instructing the Ephesian leaders, Paul kneels with the elders and prays. Emotions overcome them all. God has forged a genuine bond of love between them. They fall to their knees (a symbol of accepting the authority of a higher power) by the seashore, join hands, pray, and weep unashamedly. Then the elders escort Paul to the ship, and after a final series of embraces, they watch him go up the gangplank.

Personalize this lesson.

 Acts 20:24 could be called Paul's mission statement: *"'But I do not account my life of any value nor as precious to myself, if only I may finish my course and the ministry that I received from the Lord Jesus, to testify to the gospel of the grace of God.'"* Paul gave up a life of relative comfort, safety, and the approval of others in order to spread the news about Jesus far and wide. To him, the joy of seeing people trust Christ and the promise of a reward in heaven far outweighed what he gave up on earth.

Take some time to reflect on the "course" *you* have received from Jesus, and what it will take to finish it. What could distract you from fulfilling God's purposes for your life? How can you keep your focus on Jesus? Who might help you stay true to your calling? Commit these matters to the Lord in prayer.

Lesson 23

Into Roman Captivity
Acts 21

❖ Acts 21:1-14—Paul Visits Tyre and Caesarea

1. What does Paul do when his ship lands in Tyre?

   _____

   _____

2. How is Paul's action consistent with the rest of his life?

   _____

   _____

3. What different things happen to Paul during his stay in Tyre (either implied or clearly stated)?

   _____

   _____

   _____

4. Read Acts 21:8 and Acts 6:3-5. How would you describe Philip?

   _____

   _____

   _____

5. What do Philip's daughters do, and what does this tell you about the role of women in the early church? (See also Acts 2:17-18.)

   _____

   _____

6. With what authority does Agabus give his prophecy to Paul?

    _____

    _____

7. What does he say will happen to Paul?

    _____

    _____

8. How do the disciples react to the prophecy? How does Paul react?

    _____

    _____

9. Do you think Paul is right in his decision to go to Jerusalem after being warned by others not to? Use Scripture from Acts to support your opinion.

    _____

    _____

    _____

10. What role do emotions play in Paul's decision?

    _____

    _____

11. Compare Paul's attitude in verse 13 with Jesus' teaching in Luke 14:25-33. How does Paul live out the principles in the Luke passage?

    _____

    _____

    _____

12. What do you think the disciples mean when they say, *"Let the will of the Lord be done"* (21:14)?

    _____

    _____

❖ Acts 21:15-17—Paul Returns to Jerusalem

13. Paul concludes his third and last missionary journey. Turn to Appendix C in the back of this book and, on the map, trace this journey on with your finger. (The record of it begins in Acts 18:23.) Review the events of this journey. What do you learn about God through this account?

_____

_____

_____

14. What traits do you see that make Paul an effective leader?

_____

_____

_____

15. How are Paul and the rest of the disciples received in Jerusalem?

_____

_____

❖ Acts 21:18-26—Paul and the Jerusalem Elders

16. After greeting all the Jerusalem elders, what does Paul do, and what is the result?

_____

_____

17. What do the elders ask Paul to do for the zealous Jewish believers in Jerusalem, and why?

_____

_____

18. Do you think Paul is right or wrong in what he does? (Think back over previous lessons and other Scripture for help.)

_____

_____

❖ Acts 21:27-40—Paul Is Arrested in Jerusalem

19. Describe the events that lead to and surround Paul's arrest.

   _____

   _____

20. How is this crowd like others Paul has faced on his missionary journeys?

   _____

   _____

21. What impresses you most about Paul in this scene?

   _____

   _____

Apply what you have learned. Paul's friends in Tyre and Caesarea beg him not to go to Jerusalem, knowing that he may be imprisoned or even killed there. However, convinced the Holy Spirit is leading him to go, Paul obeys and remains resolute.

Are you trying to "protect" people you love by dissuading them from pursuing a difficult or dangerous co urse, even though they believe it is God's call for them? Or, perhaps you, like Paul, are experiencing discouragement from well-meaning friends as you try to pursue a desire God has planted in your heart.

How can Paul's example help you to navigate these difficult situations? Ask God to help you trust Him. With His help, commit yourself to encourage the ones you love to follow the Spirit's leading, even if it is not what you would choose. Or if you are the one God is leading on an uncertain path, take courage knowing that He will accompany you with His strength and peace in whatever He asks you to do.

Into Roman Captivity
Acts 21

A Week in Tyre

After recording details of the sad farewell at Miletus, Luke describes the route of his journey by sea with Paul and the other missionaries. They proceed southward along the rugged coast of Asia Minor with its many islands. At Cos, they turn from south to east, stopping first at Rhodes, then sailing on to Patara to wait for a larger vessel capable of crossing the Mediterranean. From Patara, they sail directly for Tyre, where they remain for seven days to unload cargo.

At Tyre, Paul finds a group of Christians and spends time with them, recounting his missionary activities. The church there may have been founded by Jewish Christians who fled Jerusalem after the stoning of Stephen. If so, it is ironic that Paul, the one who had caused them to flee Jerusalem, now seeks them out as fellow believers to encourage them and to be encouraged. Some people from the congregation, inspired by the Holy Spirit, urge Paul not to go to Jerusalem because he will be harmed. But Paul, convinced that the Spirit is leading him there, is determined to go regardless of the consequences. After only a week together, the believers escort Paul and his fellow missionaries to their ship, sharing goodbyes. Former strangers to one another, they had forged a bond of oneness in Christ.

Agabus Returns

Their ship sails the short distance to Ptolemais, the southernmost Phoenician harbor. (Ptolemais today is called *Acre* in English.) They arrive at Caesarea the next day. In Caesarea, Paul stays at the home of Philip the Evangelist. Philip had been appointed 20 years before as one of the seven deacons of the Jerusalem church. According to tradition,

Philip settled in Caesarea, reared his family there, and served as a faithful Christian leader in that part of the Roman Empire. Caesarea was the administrative capital of Judea and an outpost for Christianity. Philip has four daughters blessed with the gift of prophecy—which includes the ability to proclaim God's Word.

While Paul is visiting, Philip receives Agabus, a visitor from Jerusalem. Earlier in Acts, Agabus came to Antioch and foretold the famine in Judea (11:27-28). He now returns to Caesarea and predicts Paul's arrest in Jerusalem, which he emphasizes by binding Paul's hands and feet with his belt, a method used by many Old Testament prophets to illustrate their messages. Hearing Agabus's words, Luke and the rest of the company fear for Paul's life and beg him not to go. Paul is distressed by their pleading, but says he is *"ready not only to be imprisoned but even to die in Jerusalem for the name of the Lord Jesus"* (21:13). His friends accept his decision as God's will (21:14).

Welcome to Jerusalem

Paul and his company complete their 64-mile journey to Jerusalem in time for the Pentecost festivities. The Caesarean Christians had arranged for them to stay with Mnason, a man from Cyprus who had lived in Jerusalem many years. Some scholars suggest he gave Luke much of the information he needed to write the first chapters of the book of Acts.

A Visit With James

A day after their arrival, Paul and some of his company visit James, the head of the Jerusalem church. All the elders are present; however, none of the original apostles is mentioned by name. Though they had remained in Jerusalem at the beginning of the persecution, they were presumably either dead or had scattered to establish other churches. Paul reports on his missionary activities, telling them what God has done among the Gentiles. The elders praise God, but express concern about a false accusation involving Paul's teaching. They inform him that some people believe he is urging Jews to reject circumcision and the Law of Moses.

To stop the criticism, the leaders suggest that Paul perform an act of Jewish piety. They urge him to pay for the doves and lambs to be sacrificed by four needy Jewish Christians who had suffered defilement after taking a Nazirite vow. The men needed to be purified, a process that took seven days in the temple. Paul agrees to go to the temple with the men the next day to share in the period of purification. Paul is not compromising the freedom from Jewish rituals that he has in Christ, but he permits the Jews to keep aspects of their Old Testament practices such as circumcision and any laws connected with that rite. At the same time, as a mark of love, he asks Jewish believers to free Gentile Christians from the need for circumcision (15:1-2; Galatians 2:11-12). He also requests that Gentile Christians observe some basic requirements of the Law (Acts 15:28-29; Romans 14:13-15) to avoid offending others. The Lord's commandment for both Jewish and Gentile believers is the law of love (John 15:12).

Paul's Arrest

When the process of purification is nearly finished, some Jews incite a mob against Paul. Men from Asia who had harassed him throughout Asia Minor are now in Jerusalem for Pentecost. Seeing an opportunity to attack Paul, they falsely accuse him, shouting that he has defiled the holy place by taking a Gentile with him into the temple precincts. Paul knew temple Law demanded the death of a Gentile who went beyond the outer court, and he would never have violated the Law.

The mob drags Paul into the street and beats him. He is in danger of being killed when Roman soldiers rescue him. They carry him to their barracks in Fort Antonia, the Roman military headquarters in Jerusalem, and bind him in chains. Thinking they have seized an Egyptian criminal high on Rome's "Wanted List," the commander is surprised when Paul speaks to him in Greek. Paul says he is a Jew from Tarsus and asks for permission to address the crowd. When his request is granted, Paul stands on the steps, motions to the crowd with his hand, and begins speaking to the people in Hebrew, the language of the Jews. Our next lesson describes the dramatic scene that follows.

Personalize this lesson.

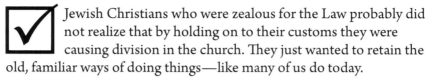 Jewish Christians who were zealous for the Law probably did not realize that by holding on to their customs they were causing division in the church. They just wanted to retain the old, familiar ways of doing things—like many of us do today.

Think about the church traditions with which you feel most comfortable: style of music, worship service format, Christian education structure, role of women in ministry, and so on. Would you be willing to let go of any of these if they proved to be a stumbling block to others, or if they were no longer effective in today's culture? Are you willing to embrace new ways of following biblical principles in your fellowship? Ask God to help you hold fast to the truths of Scripture, while holding customs and traditions with an open hand.

Farewell, Jerusalem
Acts 22

❖ Acts 22:1-5—Paul Tells of His Jewish Background

1. Read Acts 21:30–22:2. How would you describe the crowd Paul is addressing?

   _____

   _____

   _____

2. What might account for the dramatic change in the crowd?

   _____

   _____

3. More than 20 years have gone by since Paul, as a zealous Jew, persecuted the church. What details of his background would make Paul's Jewish audience identify with him?

   _____

   _____

   _____

4. What can you learn from Paul about gaining the respect of people who hold opposing views?

   _____

   _____

   _____

❖ Acts 22:6-11—Paul Speaks of His Conversion

5. What truths about God was Paul forced to recognize at the time of his conversion?

   _____

   _____

   _____

6. In the Gospel of John, Christ explains the life-changing experience of a personal encounter with God. From the following verses, what is involved in becoming a believer?

   a. John 1:12-13 _____

   _____

   _____

   b. John 3:3-18 _____

   _____

   _____

7. Have you personally "believed and received" Christ into your life while studying the book of Acts so far? Has the study brought you closer to God? If so, how?

   _____

   _____

   _____

8. What was the first question Paul asked Jesus on the Damascus road?

   _____

   _____

9. What does Paul's second question reveal about his understanding of the proper response to acknowledging Jesus as Lord? (See also James 2:14-17.)

   _____

   _____

❖ Acts 22:12-16—Paul Describes How Ananias Helped Him in Damascus

10. According to Ananias, what did God plan for Paul (verse 14)?

_____

_____

11. What is the natural result of saying "yes" to God (verses 15-16)?

_____

_____

_____

12. Review Acts 9:15-16. How is this message from Ananias good news to Paul?

_____

_____

_____

13. What is the bad news?

_____

_____

❖ Acts 22:17-21—Paul Tells the Jews About His Call to the Gentiles

14. Read Galatians 1:15-18. How much time elapsed after Paul's conversion before he returned to Jerusalem, and why is this time important?

_____

_____

_____

15. What is God's message to Paul in the trance (Acts 22:17-18)?

_____

_____

16. Why do you think Paul again mentions his persecution of the Christians?

_____

_____

❖ Acts 22:21-30—The Jews Reject Paul's Defense

17. Paul boldly states to the Jews God's command to go to the Gentiles. Why do you think he does this?

_____

_____

18. Why do the Jews suddenly become angry?

_____

_____

19. Read Exodus 34:10-16 and Leviticus 18:1-5. Why are the Jews concerned about contact with the Gentiles?

_____

_____

20. Why does God direct Paul to go to the Gentiles?

_____

_____

Apply what you have learned. When Paul addressed a hostile crowd in order to tell them about Jesus, he began by identifying with their background and values. Do you know anyone who has a negative attitude toward Christians and their faith—perhaps even toward you? Think of one such person. Now write down several things you have in common with this person: background, interests, etc. Do you share any values? Think about how you could use these similarities as a bridge to talk about spiritual matters.

Farewell, Jerusalem
Acts 22

Following his arrest, Paul has five opportunities to present Christ
to audiences of increasing prestige. He speaks first to a street crowd
assembled outside Fort Antonia; second to the religious leaders of Israel;
third before the Roman Governor Felix; fourth before Governor Festus;
and fifth before King Agrippa. Chapters 22–26 record these speeches.

From the Steps of Antonia

Standing on the steps leading up to the tower of Antonia, Rome's
military fortress on the temple square, Paul must experience mixed
emotions. His ability to stand is itself astonishing, after being cruelly
beaten by the mob near the temple. The crowd, mostly unaware of the
reason for the riot, becomes hushed when they hear Paul speaking in
Hebrew, the language of Israel.

Paul's message to the crowd has three parts. First, Paul addresses the
mob as *"Brothers and fathers"* (Acts 22:1) and tells about his early life.
He was a Jew, born in Tarsus, but raised in Jerusalem. In the school of
Gamaliel, he was trained in the Law according to its strictest meaning.
He proved his zeal for God by persecuting Christians unto death. The
high priest and high court gave him authority to track down Christians
in Damascus and bring them to Jerusalem to be punished.

In the second part of his defense, Paul recounts his conversion for the
second time (see also Acts 9 and 26). He varies each account depending
on his audience, and together they paint a complete picture of his
experience. The use of the pronoun we in chapters leading up to this
point indicates that Luke accompanied Paul and probably heard his
speech in person.

On the way to Damascus, Jesus appeared to Paul in an unmistakable way.

The brilliant light of Christ's appearing was visible to his companions, although they were unable to hear His voice. The vision occurred at noon, yet the light shining down on him was brighter than the sun, making him blind.

The crowd listens attentively as Paul describes what happened next. *"I fell to the ground and heard a voice saying to me, 'Saul, Saul, why are you persecuting Me?' And I answered, 'Who are You, Lord?' And He said to me, 'I am Jesus of Nazareth, whom you are persecuting'"* (22:7-8). Here Paul quotes Jesus' given name, a common name among Jews. Probably for this reason Paul seldom uses it alone in referring to his Lord. His account of being led to Damascus and visited by Ananias parallels Acts 9. He concludes with Ananias's charge to be baptized.

In the third part of his address, Paul includes an experience not mentioned earlier. While praying at the temple in Jerusalem, he fell into a trance and received a vision: Right in the Jewish sanctuary, Paul saw Jesus and heard Him say to him, *"Make haste and get out of Jerusalem quickly, because they will not accept your testimony about Me"* (22:18). Paul protested to the Lord because he wanted to remain in the Holy City to preach the gospel to his fellow Jewish countrymen. But the Lord told him to leave and go far away to the Gentiles. Until this point, Paul had a fully attentive audience. Now, the audience's reaction prevents Paul from completing his address.

The mention of Gentiles to the Jews of that day was like the proverbial waving of a red flag before a charging bull. Jews would throw off their cloaks and fling dust in the air—a way of expressing great emotion, grief, or anger. To the crowd, God's commission to Paul seems to call into question the uniqueness of Israel as God's people, to deny the effectiveness of the Law, and to attack Jewish reverence for the temple and all its rituals. Speaking of the Gentiles would also have reminded the Jewish audience of persecution. Ever since God's call to Abraham, Gentiles had attacked the Jews, causing bitter memories. When Paul declares that the Lord said, *"Go, for I will send you far away to the Gentiles,"* they react violently and shout, *"Away with such a fellow from the earth! For he should not be allowed to live"* (22:22).

Think about the crowd rejecting Paul's words. Did he fail in his speech to the Jews? Paul tried to make his message one the Jews could "hear," spiritually, yet he refused to retreat from what God said. Instead, he entrusted the results of his words to God. What can we learn from Paul's example?

Paul Is Questioned in the Barracks

Before the mob can seize Paul again, the commander rushes his prisoner into the barracks. He turns Paul over to the centurion for questioning under torture, as was customary with slaves and strangers. The soldiers are about to scourge Paul when he asks, as he had in Philippi under similar circumstances, why a Roman citizen should be flogged without a trial. The centurion communicates Paul's protest to the commander, who is undoubtedly shocked to learn about Paul's citizenship. No scourging takes place, but Paul remains a prisoner until the next day when he is brought before the Sanhedrin to explain the riot in the temple area.

The Advantages of Roman Citizenship

Roman citizens could not be punished without a trial. They could not be examined by scourging or be bound. Most important, they had the right to appeal to Caesar and to be tried in Rome, not unlike the modern-day change of venue to ensure a fair trial. Rome kept careful records. Soldiers who were citizens wore small metal tags (similar to "dog tags" worn by present-day military personnel), indicating Roman status. Others were given a small framed document. Paul may have had one, for his claim to Roman citizenship was never questioned. God prepared Paul for the service to which He called him. Roman citizenship was one of His provisions made far in advance. Paul's rights as a Roman citizen become his ticket for a long-dreamed-of trip to Rome, as well as his protection many times during his tumultuous years of service as God's missionary to the Gentiles.

Personalize this lesson.

 Paul, likely bruised and bleeding from his beating by the mob, asks for permission to speak to the very people who attacked him. Amazingly, he tells them about Jesus until his words invoke another near-riot. Today, most of us do not have to risk our lives to share the gospel. Still, talking about our faith can be a fearful prospect.

As you think about sharing your faith, what fears do you have? Rejection? Being thought a fool? Facing arguments to which you don't know how to respond? Reflect on how these and other fears can keep you from telling others about Jesus. Then bring these fears before the Lord in prayer. Ask Him to help you overcome them for the sake of those who do not know Him.

Difficulty and Encouragement
Acts 23

Memorize God's Word: Philippians 3:20.

❖ Acts 23:1-5—Paul Addresses the Jewish Leaders

1. Rewrite Paul's opening sentence to the chief priests and Sanhedrin in your own words.

   _____

   _____

   _____

2. Paul was not sinless; therefore, how do you explain his claim to have a clear conscience? (See also 1 Corinthians 4:4; 1 John 1:9.)

   _____

   _____

3. Read Romans 3:21-26 and 8:1-4. How might these verses help someone who is struggling with guilt?

   _____

   _____

4. Read Matthew 23:27-28 and Ezekiel 13:10-16. Why do you think Paul refers to Ananias as a *"whitewashed wall"* (23:3)?

   _____

   _____

   _____

5. Read Leviticus 19:15 and Deuteronomy 25:1-2. Why does Paul accuse Ananias of behaving contrary to the Law?

    _____

    _____

6. What do you learn from the way Paul reacts when he is corrected by those nearby (23:4-5)?

    _____

    _____

    _____

❖ Acts 23:6-10—Paul Stirs Up Controversy

7. What do the Pharisees and Sadducees disagree about?

    _____

    _____

8. Why do you think Paul mentions this volatile, divisive subject?

    _____

    _____

9. How would you describe the character of the Jewish leaders?

    _____

    _____

❖ Acts 23:11—God Encourages Paul

10. When does the Lord encourage Paul?

    _____

    _____

11. What attributes of God do you see here?

    _____

    _____

    _____

12. How would you define the word *courage*? You may want to refer to a dictionary.

_____

_____

13. What do you think the Lord means when He commands Paul to "*take courage*" (23:11)?

_____

_____

14. Read Joshua 1:1-9. What insights about becoming a courageous person do you find?

_____

_____

15. What situations are you facing in which you need the Lord's encouragement? How do the verses in Joshua speak to you?

_____

_____

❖ Acts 23:12-24—The Jews Unsuccessfully Plot Against Paul

16. How do the Jews show the depth of their anger toward Paul?

_____

_____

17. What are at least two things each of the following verses teach about anger?

    a. Ephesians 4:26-27 _____

    _____

    _____

    b. James 1:19-20 _____

    _____

    _____

18. Which of the verses above do you find most meaningful, and why?

_____

_____

_____

19. How does God protect Paul from the Jews' plot?

_____

_____

❖ Acts 23:25-35—Paul Is Sent to Felix, Governor of Judea

20. Use verses from Acts 21:31-23:35 to describe Claudius Lysias, the Roman commander.

_____

_____

21. Which of his character qualities do you most admire?

_____

_____

_____

Apply what you have learned. It may seem surprising to us that religious leaders could be so upset about Paul's teaching that they would plot to kill him. Yet anger is a powerful force that, if unchecked, can lead to sin. Paul wrote to the Ephesians, *"Let all bitterness and wrath and anger and clamor and slander be put away from you, along with all malice"* (Ephesians 4:31). Ask the Lord to show you if you are harboring anger toward anyone. Is there anyone you need to forgive? If so, let go of your anger toward that person. Ask God to help you with the difficult work of forgiveness.

Difficulty and Encouragement
Acts 23

An Attempt Backfires

The Sanhedrin—the governing religious body of Jerusalem and the highest municipal council the Jews are allowed to have—falls under Roman authority. The commander values it as a fact-finding board and brings Paul before it for questioning. Addressing the Sanhedrin as brothers, he claims innocence of any wrongdoing. His attitude infuriates the high priest, Ananias, who orders those nearby to hit Paul on the mouth. Paul responds by calling him a *"whitewashed wall"* (Acts 23:3) and accusing him of violating the legal procedures he has a duty to enforce. The men standing near Paul question him for daring to revile the high priest, and Paul replies, *"I did not know, brothers, that he was the high priest"* (23:5).

Paul's reply puzzles some commentators, who think Paul means to imply irony: *"How could a high priest act in a manner so unworthy?"* Others feel Paul's poor eyesight keeps him from recognizing Ananias as the high priest. Another suggests it was not a regular meeting of the tribunal; therefore, Ananias is not wearing his identifiable priestly robes. Paul quickly apologizes, showing respect for the position of authority even though the man occupying the office seems unworthy of respect. His attitude is consistent with his teaching: *"Let every person be subject to the governing authorities"* (Romans 13:1).

Paul knows he won't benefit from the Sanhedrin's deliberation. He sees that the court, though it consists mainly of Sadducees, has a strong minority of Pharisees. He tells the assembly he is a Pharisee and that he is being tried because of his belief in the resurrection of the dead. Paul's reason for saying this is unclear. He probably hopes the Pharisees will ensure him a fair hearing because they share his belief in resurrection.

Or, he may be taking the opportunity to speak of the Resurrection before the Sadducees, who do not believe in supernatural events or beings other than God. It is also conceivable that he *intends* to provoke conflict among the differing groups.

As some of the Pharisees defend Paul, the atmosphere grows so violent that Claudius Lysias, the commander, orders his soldiers to take Paul to the fortress of Antonia for his own safety. Now the true nature of the Sanhedrin is revealed to the commander, who is more convinced than ever of Paul's innocence.

Encouragement—and a Plot

Paul may well be concerned about his fate in Jerusalem, especially after receiving repeated warnings along the way. But the following night he receives encouragement from the Lord: *"The Lord stood by him and said, 'Take courage, for as you have testified to the facts about me in Jerusalem, so you must testify also in Rome'"* (Acts 23:11). Reflecting on God's special appearance to him that night undoubtedly comforts Paul in the anxious years to come.

Think about Jesus' presence in the life of a believer. He has promised to be with us always, even to the end of the age (Matthew 28:20). He knows when we need extra encouragement, comfort, direction, or a warning, and he has any number of ways of communicating that to us. It may not always be dream or vision (though it could be!). His presence may come through Scripture, a song, the words of a friend or His "still, small voice." But He will not leave you alone to figure things out or cope by yourself. Look for Him. Call out to Him. He promises to be there for you.

Paul's enemies plot to kill him. Forty assassins begin a "hunger strike" as an incentive to hunt Paul until he is dead. They arrange for the Sanhedrin to ask Claudius Lysias for another meeting, planning to murder Paul as he travels to the gathering. But Paul's nephew hears of the plot and notifies the commander.

We know nothing else about this nephew. Some commentators think he was a disbelieving Jew, otherwise he would not have heard of the plot. But whatever the case, his family loyalty to Paul is great enough for him to risk his life. If his part in Paul's escape is discovered, he will be killed. When Claudius hears of the plot he takes immediate steps; Paul is a Roman citizen whose life must be guarded. He is kept in protective custody and sent to Caesarea by night under heavy guard.

One Step Closer to Rome

Armed troops leave with Paul for Jerusalem at nine in the evening, likely reaching Antipatris, about 35 miles from Caesarea, by dawn. The infantry returns to Jerusalem while the cavalry accompanies Paul to Caesarea, arriving that evening.

The prisoner is handed over to Felix, the procurator (governor) in Caesarea, along with a letter from Claudius. Governor Felix asks which province Paul is from, perhaps planning to turn him over to the authorities of that province. But when Paul answers, "Cilicia," Felix realizes it is not a separate province, but a territory supervised by Syria. In Cilicia they won't be bothered with such a minor Judean problem. Felix decides to hear the case himself as soon as the prosecutors from Jerusalem arrive. Once more Paul finds himself held prisoner, this time in the palace built by Herod the Great. Evidence suggests that Paul was shown every courtesy and enjoyed all the comforts of the palace for the next two years.

Think about the benefits found in difficult times. Tremendous growth can result when we persevere in obedience despite dark days, unanswered prayers, and unfulfilled hopes. If we are open to receiving whatever God offers, He grants comfort, courage, and coping power. Help that may not come how or when we desire—Paul went through anxious hours and long nights—but God always comes through. *"The surpassing power belongs to God and not to us. We are afflicted in every way, but not crushed; perplexed, but not driven to despair; persecuted, but not forsaken; struck down, but not destroyed"* (2 Corinthians 4:7-9).

Personalize this lesson.

☑ Paul wrote in Philippians 3:20 that our true citizenship is in heaven. To the Colossians he wrote, *"Seek the things that are above, where Christ is .... Set your minds on things that are above, not on things that are on earth"* (Colossians 3:1-2). This mindset helped Paul to endure mistreatment and suffering. His mind and heart were set on his calling from God, not earthly goals or desires. This attitude runs counter to our me-first, comfort-oriented culture. How can we shift our focus to heaven?

Honestly assess what you have been seeking this week, and what you have set your mind on. When is it easiest to focus on Jesus? When are you most easily distracted? What are the Lord's chief rivals for your attention? Take time to reflect on Colossians 3:1-2. What does it look like to live out this charge in your daily life? How can you continue to renew your mind (Romans 12:1-2) and grow in focus on Him and His kingdom? Ask God to show you ways to set your eyes on Him this week and believe He will draw near to you as you do!

False Charges and a Clear Conscience
Acts 22

Memorize God's Word: Philippians 3:20.

❖ Acts 24:1-9—The Jerusalem Delegation Presents Charges Against Paul in Judea

1. Ananias, the high priest; some elders; and Tertullus, the spokesman, make up the Jerusalem delegation. How would you describe their attitude toward Felix?

   _____

   _____

   _____

2. What four charges does Tertullus give against Paul?

   _____

   _____

   _____

   _____

❖ Acts 24:10-21—Paul Gives His Defense

3. According to verse 10, what is Paul's frame of mind when beginning his defense?

   _____

   _____

   _____

4. Based on the following verses, how do you think Paul can be cheerful in this situation?

   a. 2 Corinthians 4:16-18 _____

   _____

   b. Philippians 4:11-13_____

   _____

5. What reasons does Paul give for going to Jerusalem?

   _____

   _____

6. Look up the word *conscience* in a dictionary and define it.

   _____

7. From the following verses, how can we keep our consciences clear?

   a. 2 Corinthians 1:12 _____

   _____

   b. Hebrews 13:18 _____

   _____

8. What are Paul's answers to the charges the Jews make in Acts 24:5-6 (24:11-21)? (You may want to use a dictionary for insight into the charges.)

   a. Promoter of riots among the Jews_____

   _____

   _____

   b. Ringleader of the Nazarene sect_____

   _____

   _____

   c. Desecrater of the temple_____

   _____

   _____

9. Paul says the real reason the Jews are putting him on trial is the issue of the resurrection of the dead. Why is the matter so important (Romans 1:4-6)?

_____

_____

_____

❖ Acts 24:22-23—Paul Is Placed in Custody

10. What kind of knowledge does Felix have of the Way?

_____

_____

11. Paul's living conditions are decent while he awaits trial. He has freedom and friends are allowed to care for his needs. Who are Paul's friends in Caesarea (21:8-14)?

_____

_____

_____

❖ Acts 24:24-27—Paul Witnesses to Felix While in Custody

12. How long is Paul in custody under Felix?

_____

13. Why does Felix postpone making a decision about Paul?

_____

_____

_____

14. What does Paul discuss with Felix and his wife?

_____

_____

_____

15. What do you learn about witnessing from Paul's example with
    Felix?

    _____

    _____

    _____

    _____

16. Do you see progression in Felix's attitude toward spiritual
    things? Why or why not?

    _____

    _____

    _____

    _____

Apply what you have learned. Paul declared,
*"I always take pains to have a clear conscience toward
both God and man"* (Acts 24:16). How do you keep
your conscience clear? From observing Paul's life, what have
you learned about keeping a clear conscience? Describe how
a Christian can live free from a guilty conscience. Use any
Scriptures that are helpful.

False Charges and a Clear Conscience
Acts 22

Tertullus Accuses

Ananias and some elders from the Sanhedrin arrive in Caesarea five days after Paul. They are accompanied by their legal consultant, Tertullus, who becomes the Sanhedrin's spokesman for the prosecution because of his familiarity with the Roman judicial procedure. Tertullus begins his speech by lavishing praise on Felix, and ends by accusing Paul of being a troublemaker—an instigator of riots among Jews all over the world, a ringleader of the Nazarene sect, and a would-be desecrater of the temple. He says the Jews had wanted to judge Paul according to their law, but Lysias had taken him out of their hands and ordered the accusers to appear before the governor. (This information is from 6b-8a, found in text notes in some versions of the Bible.) The accusers want Felix to question Paul about these charges. The rest of the visitors from Jerusalem join in the accusations.

Felix Listens to Paul

Speaking courteously but without flattery, Paul respectfully acknowledges that Felix has years of experience in the region. He implies that this will enable Felix to judge fairly, so he, Paul, will *"cheerfully"* make his defense (Acts 24:10). Paul's choice of the word *cheerfully* reflects confidence and joy. He denies the accusations against him, saying he had been in Jerusalem no more than 12 days and had no time to organize an insurrection even if he had wanted to. He went to Jerusalem to celebrate Pentecost and to bring offerings. He had neither engaged in arguments nor stirred up a crowd; his behavior had been quiet, reverent, and orthodox. He belongs to a group called the Way, which is not a cult. The people of the Way worship the God of the fathers who has revealed Himself in the Old Testament. Together with the Pharisees, Paul believes in *"a resurrection of both the just and the unjust"* (24:15). He has always taken pains to have a clear conscience before God and people (24:16).

Think about Paul's assertion that he strove to keep a clear conscience before God and people. He could make such a declaration because he had been forgiven and cleansed by Christ: *"Christ Jesus came into the world to save sinners, of whom I am the foremost. But I received mercy for this reason, that in me, as the foremost, Jesus Christ might display His perfect patience as an example to those who were to believe in Him for eternal life"* (1 Timothy 1:15-16).

Paul trusted in Christ's righteousness; he did not strive to achieve his own righteousness by diligent adherence to the Law. His clear conscience was based on his faith in Christ and displayed none of the proud arrogance of the Jews, who relied on their own abilities to keep the Law. The New Testament is clear: We are saved by faith in Christ alone. However, our response toward this unmerited grace is to strive for holy living.

Paul states that he fully accepts the Law and the Prophets and took the Nazirite vow as an orthodox Jew, an action proving his orthodoxy. Then he repeats the charge he wants these men to discuss: *"It is with respect to the resurrection of the dead that I am on trial before you this day"* (Acts 24:21). Ananias is a Sadducee, and Paul is convinced the Sadducees are trying to separate Jewish Christians from the Jewish religion. If the Romans can be convinced that Christianity is an unauthorized religion, the church will be subject to persecution, not just from the Jews, but from the Romans as well. (From Nero's time until the reign of Constantine 200 years later, Rome inflicted terrible suffering on the church.)

The early church does not want to be severed from its roots in Judaism prematurely. Thus, Paul struggles to maintain the perception that Christianity is a legitimate fulfillment of Judaism. In the end, his view prevails, and Rome protects the fledgling church until the new movement grows and eventually threatens the Empire.

Felix's Verdict

Felix, quite familiar with the division in Judaism over the doctrine of the resurrection from the dead, postpones the case. He offers the excuse that he will have to wait to hear evidence from Lysias before passing judgment, a hearing that evidently never takes place. But Felix is still interested in his prisoner for another reason. Recently, he had married a young princess, Drusilla, one of three daughters of King Herod Agrippa I. Drusilla had left her first husband, Azizus, Syrian king of Enesa, to marry Felix, and was his third wife; their son, also named Agrippa, died in the eruption of Mount Vesuvius.

After hearing of Paul, Drusilla is curious and wishes an audience with him. Felix orders Paul be brought to the court chamber to speak with her. Paul begins a conversation on righteousness, self-control, and the judgment to come. However, Felix, remembering his own past actions, finds the ethical implications of the Christian faith too personally convicting. He interrupts the talk, saying he will call for Paul to return at a more convenient time.

Felix has many private talks with Paul. Acts 24:26 states he sent for him often, hinting to Paul that a bribe to gain his freedom would be acceptable. Felix may think Paul has access to financial resources or that he can call on his Nazarene friends to supply them. Paul refuses to be part of such an arrangement, so Felix keeps Paul in custody, his case unsettled, for the remaining two years of his term of office. If he is unable to extract a bribe from Paul, then he will do the politically expedient thing and please the Jews by keeping him a prisoner. To his credit, he does arrange for Paul to have good treatment and allows him unlimited visitors.

Think about Felix's interest in Paul. Felix was a man who thought about and discussed spiritual matters, but never arrived at a decision. For two years he continued to send for Paul—probably to hint for a bribe. Paul would have seized every opportunity to present Christ, but Felix, like many today, was willing to discuss religion, but reluctant to act. He failed to make the most important decision a person will ever make—to trust oneself to Christ. What are some reasons that an individual might feel hesitant to commit to Christ? How can you respond with wisdom and sensitivity to the questions of someone who is seeking like Felix?

Personalize this lesson.

 Paul provides an example of faithful patience while in a position of waiting. It must have been difficult for the fiery, driven apostle to stay in Felix's prison for two years, his ministry on hold indefinitely. Yet it was part of God's plan.

In what areas of your life are you waiting for God to work? Ask God to help you grow in trust that His plan and His timing are perfect. Look for ways to serve Him while you wait. Take advantage of this waiting time to learn, grow in character, and rest to prepare for what God has for you next.

Witness and Verdict
Acts 25–26

Memorize God's Word: Hebrews 11:6.

❖ Acts 25:1-12—Paul Appeals to Rome

1. Why does Festus want to hold Paul's trial in Jerusalem?

    _____

    _____

2. Festus seeks to please people; Paul seeks to please God. What
    do the following verses say about living to please the Lord rather
    than living to please others?

    a. Proverbs 1:7 _____

        _____

    b. 2 Corinthians 5:9-10 _____

        _____

3. Why do you think Paul appeals to Caesar?

    _____

    _____

❖ Acts 25:13-27—Festus Discusses Paul's Case With King Agrippa

4. What does Festus find puzzling about Paul's case?

    _____

    _____

5. What does Festus want King Agrippa to do in this meeting with Paul?

_____

_____

❖ Acts 26:1-15—Paul Defends Himself Before King Agrippa

6. Review Acts 21:28 and the original charges the Jews make against Paul. How does Paul defend himself to Agrippa against the Jews' charges?

_____

_____

_____

7. Why does Paul consider himself *"fortunate"* (26:2) in making his defense to Agrippa?

_____

_____

_____

8. The word *goad* means *a pointed rod used to urge on or guide an animal.* What do you think Jesus means when He says Paul is kicking *"against the goads"* (26:14)?

_____

_____

_____

❖ Acts 26:16-23—Paul Describes His God-Given Ministry

9. What was Jesus' purpose in appearing to Paul?

_____

_____

_____

10. What does God want to do in the lives of the Gentiles (Acts 26:17-18)?

God proposes to:	Meaning:
a.	
b.	
c.	
d.	
e.	

11. How did Paul respond to the vision?

_____

_____

12. Which three specific things do you find most noteworthy in Paul's defense to King Agrippa (Acts 26:19-23)?

_____

_____

_____

❖ Acts 26:24-32—Agrippa Acknowledges Paul's Innocence

13. From this chapter, describe each person's attitude toward God.

a. Paul _____

_____

b. Festus _____

_____

   c. Agrippa _____

_____

14. In verse 29, Paul tells Agrippa and all the audience how important it is for each of them to become a Christian. Why do you think Paul does this?

_____

_____

_____

15. What is Agrippa's verdict regarding Paul?

_____

_____

Apply what you have learned. Six chapters of Acts detail Paul's trials. Throughout, Paul is falsely accused, imprisoned without cause, and treated unjustly. Yet he continually models Jesus' charge to *"Love your enemies and pray for those who persecute you"* (Matthew 5:44). He defends himself, but his focus is on persuading his persecutors to believe in Jesus (Acts 26:29).

Do you have any enemies? Is there anyone who routinely treats you rudely or unfairly? If you are not already doing so, make a plan to pray for that person regularly. Ask God to work in that person's heart and reveal His love to them!

Witness and Verdict
Acts 25–26

The Changing of the Guard

Porcius Festus, the proconsul replacing Felix, is from a well-known family with senatorial rank. Shortly after arriving in his province, sometime in AD 60, he tours and inspects Jerusalem. He is met by the high priests and the Sanhedrin, who tell him of Paul's case, hoping the inexperienced Festus will send Paul to Jerusalem for trial. They have plans to ambush and kill Paul on his way there. Instead, Festus invites them to go to Caesarea with him and state their case against Paul. Once there, the Sanhedrin hurls unproven accusations at the apostle, who refutes them.

Festus is confronted with the same problem Felix had been unable to solve: Should he release Paul, an innocent man, or appease the Sanhedrin by sending him to Jerusalem? Wanting to do the Jews a favor at the beginning of his term of office, Festus asks Paul if he is willing to stand trial in Jerusalem. But Paul knows too well how dangerous standing trial in Jerusalem would be for him and states that he wants to be tried in Caesar's court. After consulting with his council, Festus replies, *"To Caesar you have appealed; to Caesar you shall go"* (Acts 25:12). The arrangement relieves Festus of having to decide between the two parties and allows Paul a way of getting to Rome, the objective of his dreams.

Agrippa Visits Caesarea

Before Paul leaves for Rome, Festus entertains King Agrippa and his sister, Bernice, both great-grandchildren of Herod the Great, the builder of the glorious temple in Jerusalem. Their brother-sister relationship is questionable; she is his consort at all state functions, assuming the position of queen on ceremonial occasions. Their younger sister i married to Felix. Agrippa's domain at this time includes major portions of Palestine. (Later he will be given supervision of the temple and the authority to appoint high priests.)

The relationship between king and proconsul is an interesting one. Rome maintains ultimate control and authority through the proconsul, and delegates ceremonial responsibilities and considerable authority to local kings or other state officials. Judea is one of the less reliable areas of the far-flung Empire; the administrative functions of government take place in Caesarea rather than the more volatile city of Jerusalem.

King Agrippa is well acquainted with religious conditions in Jerusalem and surrounding areas. Bernice, known for her frivolity and beauty, has an unsavory moral reputation, though outwardly she displays interest in religion, and even took a Nazirite vow at one stage. Agrippa and Bernice spend several days in Caesarea, and Festus—knowing very little about Jewish religion and practices—takes advantage of the opportunity to consult the king about Paul's case.

Honored With a Royal Audience

Agrippa expresses interest in the case and wants to see Paul for himself. Festus arranges to meet the next day, assembling a group of high-ranking military and leading men of the city. The group, together with Agrippa and Bernice in their finest royal robes, creates a spectacle as they march with great pomp and ceremony into the court chamber of Herod's palace to question Paul.

For a third time, Paul finds himself recounting his conversion. In his first account (Acts chapter 9), Paul emphasized Jesus' extraordinary appearance to him, which gave him authority equal to that of the 12 apostles. In his second account (Acts chapter 22), Paul proclaimed he was set aside to be God's witness. Now, in his final account, Paul emphasizes his call to preach to the Gentiles.

Paul begins his defense by crediting Agrippa with a thorough knowledge ⸱⸱he customs and controversies of the Jews. He then bases his defense ⸱truths: He is a loyal Jew; he believes Holy Scripture; and he ⸱ to direct revelation from God. Paul first states that he ⸱ belonging to the strictest party of Judaism. Then ⸱l vigorously opposed those who believed in enemies of God. He recounts his conversion experience, describing how God's glory overtook him at noon as he came to Damascus. Jesus had said to Paul, *"It is hard for you to kick against the goads"* (Acts 26:14). After Paul called the crucified One *"Lord"* (26:15), Jesus appointed him to witness to the Gentiles.

Think about Jesus' words to Saul: *"It is hard for you to kick against the goads"* (26:14). A goad is a prod used to guide animals in the right direction. We can imagine that God was prodding Paul to accept the truth of the gospel.

How can we be sure we are not resisting the prodding of the Holy Spirit? First, any thoughts or plans we might have will be consistent with the whole teaching of Scripture. Second, as we pray and seek to be open to God, we will have inner peace and a yielded will. Third, we will become aware of a desire to glorify Jesus and to help in the work of His kingdom. If we are on the wrong track—as Paul was—God will stop us. If we are open to His leading and spending time in His Word, He promises, *"I will instruct you and teach you in the way you should go; I will counsel you with My eye upon you"* (Psalm 32:8).

Paul appeals to Agrippa as one Jew to another, stating that it would be wrong to disobey a message from heaven. He points out that Jewish prophets predicted Christ's death and resurrection. At this point, Festus interrupts to accuse Paul of being mad. Paul defends his sanity and calls on Agrippa to affirm the fulfilled prophecy. He asks Agrippa, *"Do you believe the prophets?"* (26:27). But Agrippa will not be persuaded to become a Christian. Paul states his earnest desire for Agrippa and the others to believe. The review ends as the king rises to leave the assembly. Both the king and proconsul later agree that Paul is innocent, but because Paul has appealed to Caesar, Festus cannot declare him innocent without detracting from the emperor's prestige.

Personalize this lesson.

☑ Jesus sent Paul to the Gentiles *"to open their eyes, so that they may turn from darkness to light and from the power of Satan to God, that they may receive forgiveness of sins and a place among those who are sanctified by faith in Me"* (Acts 26:17-18). Because of God's mercy, we can receive each of these immeasurable gifts. Reflect on each of the phrases of God's plan for believers. How have you seen Him fulfill each of these promises in your life? Spend some time in praise and worship, thanking Him for what He has done for you.

God Will Take Care of You
Acts 27

❖ Acts 27:1-8—Paul Begins to Sail to Rome

1. Summarize what happened on the first segment of the sea voyage. Locate the ports mentioned on the map in the appendix.

    _____

    _____

    _____

2. a. Which friend accompanies Paul on this journey?

    _____

    b. What do you learn about friendship from the examples of these two men? (See also Colossians 4:10, 14; Philemon 23-24.)

    _____

    _____

3. What do the following verses have to say about friendship?
    a. Proverbs 17:17 _____

    _____

    b. Proverbs 18:24 _____

    _____

    c. Proverbs 27:5-6 _____

    _____

4. Read John 15:12-17. What do you learn about the ultimate
    friendship from these verses? How did Luke (and others
    who may have traveled with Paul) demonstrate this kind of
    friendship?

    _____

    _____

    _____

❖ Acts 27:9-20—Caught in a Winter Storm

5. Read 2 Corinthians 11:25-26. What in Paul's background
    enables him to advise the centurion, pilot, and ship owner to
    stop the voyage?

    _____

    _____

6. What decision do those in charge make?

    _____

    _____

❖ Acts 27:21-26—Paul Encourages the Crew

7. Considering all that Paul says in Acts 27:21-26 to the people
    aboard ship, why do you think he begins his talk with, *"Men, you
    should have listened to me"* (27:21)?

    _____

    _____

8. What is the basis of Paul's encouraging words to his shipmates?

    _____

    _____

9. Why does Paul know He can rely on what God told him? (See
    Psalm 33:4.)

    _____

    _____

❖ Acts 27:27-44—Paul Provides Leadership

10. What evidence do you find in these verses that Paul's witness about God has an impact on the crew?

_____

_____

_____

11. How is Paul's life threatened once again?

_____

_____

12. How is he protected?

_____

_____

13. How is God's prior word to Paul fulfilled (Acts 27:23-26)?

_____

_____

14. Imagine that you are one of the people who began this voyage with no personal knowledge of God and you survived the shipwreck. Imagine how the storm felt, looked, and sounded. What emotions do you experience? How do you feel about Paul? About God?

_____

_____

_____

15. Read through Acts 27 again and list at least five different qualities of Paul's leadership.

_____

_____

_____

_____

16. Which one of these qualities do you find most admirable? Why?

_____

_____

_____

_____

Apply what you have learned. In the crisis at sea, Paul demonstrates two notable aspects of leadership: He encourages others to trust in God's promise, and he offers ideas to change the situation. Think of a dilemma your church or ministry is currently facing. How might you take one or both of these steps in regard to this situation? Ask God what He wants you to do to help, and then make a plan to act.

God Will Take Care of You
Acts 27

In this chapter, Luke resumes his use of the pronoun *we*, not used since the account of Paul's days in Jerusalem. *"We"* probably includes others besides Luke and Paul. During Paul's two years in Caesarea, Luke may have remained in the background, possibly writing the third Gospel or gathering material for the book of Acts. Commentators and marine experts recognize Luke's account of the voyage from Caesarea to Rome as perhaps the best description available of ancient navigation.

Ready for a Sea Voyage

A ship anchored at Caesarea is scheduled to sail toward Rome. Paul begins his voyage on this ship, but will change ships frequently on his way to Rome. A centurion named Julius guards Paul throughout his journey. The centurion, who treats Paul with courtesy, allows him to go ashore at Sidon, where there is a flourishing church.

From Sidon, westerly winds make it dangerous for the ship to sail its natural course—directly south and west of Cyprus. Instead, the ship travels close to the shore near Cilicia and Pamphylia, sailing east and north of Cyprus, protected from the prevailing wind. It takes 15 days to reach Myra in Lycia, one of the chief ports used in Egyptian trade. Paul and his companions transfer to a ship that carries 276 people, including passengers and crew, and a cargo of wheat from Alexandria.

The ship cannot follow the usual route to Rome because of weather conditions in the early fall. Progress is slow heading for Cnidus, the southwest point of Asia Minor. Beyond Cnidus, the ship has no more land breeze to aid its progress. The open Aegean Sea lies to their north. Unable to make headway directly into the strong west wind, the vessel is driven south, passing Mount Salome on the eastern tip of Crete.

They reach Fair Havens on the south coast of the island. Unfortunately, the bay there is too exposed to allow the ship to winter. Navigation is considered dangerous from about September 14 to about November 11. After that time, all sailing is completely suspended until March 5. The crew and passengers face a dilemma.

A Gambler's Chance

To go directly to Italy is impossible. Paul—now quite an experienced sailor—strongly advises against leaving Fair Havens, but the majority aboard decide to take a chance on reaching Phoenix, 30 miles away. They have scarcely left port when a storm strikes so violently that they have to let themselves drift. Soon they pass by the small island of Cauda. The ship has developed dangerous leaks from the storm's battering, so they strengthen it by tying ropes around it. To keep from drifting into the graveyard of ships on the shoals of Syrtis Major, a drag anchor is lowered to act as a brake. The next day, the crew begins throwing cargo into the sea to lighten the ship. On the third day, the passengers help toss the ship's tackle overboard. As the storm continues, hope of survival grows dimmer. For several days they see neither sun nor stars, and the storm intensifies. All hope of being saved seems lost.

When in the Hour of Deepest Need

Luke probably does not have a word for seasickness, saying only that they go without food for a long time. Then Paul speaks to the captain and the crew: If they had listened to him, these things would not have happened, but there is still reason for them to be of good courage. He says that an *"angel of God to whom I belong and whom I worship"* appeared to him and said that he will stand before Caesar, and that God will save everyone on the ship along with him, although the ship will be lost. Paul tells them that he relies on God's promise.

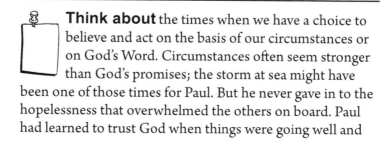

Think about the times when we have a choice to believe and act on the basis of our circumstances or on God's Word. Circumstances often seem stronger than God's promises; the storm at sea might have been one of those times for Paul. But he never gave in to the hopelessness that overwhelmed the others on board. Paul had learned to trust God when things were going well and when things were going badly. He had exercised his faith, and it grew strong. What opportunities do you have now to grow in faith.

Approaching Land

For two weeks the storm tosses the ship around in the waters between Crete, Sicily, and Malta. The distance in a straight line from Fair Havens to Malta is 625 miles; the ordeal this ship endures is amazing. Sometime during the 14th night, the sailors think they hear the sound of a distant breaker and assume they are running aground as Paul had predicted. When soundings confirm this, anchors are set, and some of the seamen lower the small lifeboat on board into the water. They plan to abandon ship and let the passengers fend for themselves. Paul realizes what is happening and knows that unless the crew stays with the ship, no one will be saved. He warns the soldiers, who keep the sailors on board by cutting the ropes holding the lifeboat. The sailors have no choice now but to ground the ship to get ashore—a big step of faith. Again, Paul says that all will be well and tells them to eat something. He takes some bread and gives thanks to God publicly. The others are encouraged and follow his example.

All Land Safely

The next morning they decide to try beaching the ship, so they cast off the anchors. They run into a sandbar; the bow wedges in the sand, and waves batter the stern. The soldiers know they are responsible for delivering the prisoners to Rome; if any escape, the soldiers can be executed for negligence of duty. They plan to kill the prisoners to prevent their escape, but Julius stops them because he wants to save Paul. He commands everyone to jump overboard, first those who can swim, then the others, who could grab wreckage from the ship and manage as best they can. Eventually, all of them reach land.

Personalize this lesson.

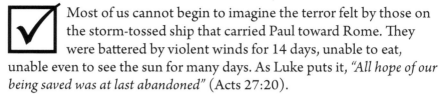 Most of us cannot begin to imagine the terror felt by those on the storm-tossed ship that carried Paul toward Rome. They were battered by violent winds for 14 days, unable to eat, unable even to see the sun for many days. As Luke puts it, *"All hope of our being saved was at last abandoned"* (Acts 27:20).

Paul shared the same desperate circumstances. Yet his faith in God apparently kept him calm and level-headed. This calm enabled him to make suggestions that ultimately saved the lives of all aboard. His response to the situation no doubt displayed the power of God to everyone on the ship.

How we respond in a crisis can be a good measure of our faith. Is our initial response to frightening circumstances panic or trust? Think about the last crisis you faced and your response. Were you able to trust God as much as you would like? If not, ask God to show you how you can grow in faith and be a witness to others by staying calm when trouble threatens.

Paul in Rome
Acts 28

❖ Acts 28:1-10—Paul Is Shipwrecked on Malta

1. How would you describe the inhabitants of the island?

    _____

    _____

2. What is their first impression of Paul?

    _____

3. How does their impression of Paul change?

    _____

    _____

4. Reread Acts 28:1-10, remembering that God loves the people of
    Malta and wants to reveal Christ to them. What did God do to
    reveal Himself to them? Try to list at least five things.

    _____

    _____

    _____

    _____

    _____

❖ Acts 28:11-16—Paul Arrives in Rome

5. How long is Paul on Malta?

    _____

6. Which part or place on this voyage to Rome stands out most to you, and why?

_____

_____

_____

_____

7. How do you think Paul might be feeling as he approaches Rome, and what effect does the Romans' ministry have on him?

_____

_____

_____

❖ Acts 28:17-22—Paul Meets With the Jewish Leaders in Rome

8. How long does Paul wait before he contacts the Jewish leaders?

_____

9. How might Paul have used this time?

_____

_____

10. What are four main points of Paul's first message to them?

_____

_____

_____

_____

11. What plan for reaching the Jews do you see in the way Paul begins his relationship with these leaders?

_____

_____

_____

❖ Acts 28:23-28—Paul Preaches Christ to the Jewish Leaders in Rome

12. What reasoning does Paul use to try to convince his Jewish audience about Jesus?

_____

_____

_____

13. How do the Jews react to Paul's message?

_____

_____

14. How does Paul deal with those who do not believe, and what do you learn from this?

_____

_____

_____

❖ Acts 28:30-31—Paul Ministers an Additional Two Years in Rome

15. Describe Paul's living conditions in Rome. (Refer also to other verses in this chapter.)

_____

_____

_____

16. How does Paul use his time during these years?

_____

_____

17. How does the Roman government's attitude toward Paul affect his ministry?

_____

_____

18. Read 2 Timothy 4. Most scholars agree that Paul wrote
    2 Timothy during a later, second imprisonment in Rome.
    The letter is also thought to be his last written words. He was
    convinced his execution would happen soon. What can you
    learn about Paul's spiritual condition at the end of his life from
    this chapter?

    _____

    _____

    _____

    _____

19. What impresses you the most about Paul's last words in
    2 Timothy 4?

    _____

    _____

    _____

    _____

Apply what you have learned. Think back
over Paul's life described in Acts 9:1-31 and Acts
13-30. What stands out to you most about Paul and
his ministry? What did Paul do—or not do—that most
challenges you? What would you most like to emulate
about the way he lived his life? Choose the lesson from Paul
you most want to take away, and write your own personal
application. What will you do as a result of this study?

Paul in Rome
Acts 28

The Fire and the Serpent

Paul's ill-fated journey by sea probably began about mid-November and ended 14 days later. Upon reaching the shore, the travelers discover they are on the island of Malta. Malta has an important seaport, but the voyagers land far from the large harbor, in what is known today as Saint Paul's Bay.

The natives' Phoenician dialect is not too different from Aramaic, so Paul is able to communicate with them. They build a fire for the exhausted voyagers, who warm up and dry themselves. Paul, not one to stand around when there is work to do, gathers up an armful of sticks to fuel the fire. He inadvertently picks up a poisonous snake. The superstitious islanders think Paul must be a murderer, and justice is now demanding his death. They wait expectantly for him to die from the snake bite, but when Paul is unharmed and shakes the snake off into the fire, they decide he must be a god. Paul corrects them: God alone is worthy of their worship.

Think about the people of Malta believing that if a snake had bitten Paul, he must have deserved it. Many feel misfortune comes as a result of sin. Sometimes that holds true, but we ought to be very careful about making those judgments. Suffering people need our compassion, not our chiding. If God has any lessons to teach a hurting person, He is capable of doing so without our help.

Close to the little bay where Paul and his fellow travelers land is the estate of Publius, *"the chief man of the island"* (28:7). Publius opens his home to some of the voyagers, including Luke and Paul. Publius's father is ill with fever and dysentery; Paul prays for him, and he is healed. Word of Paul's power spreads rapidly, and sick people come from all over the island to be healed. Luke doesn't mention Paul preaching on Malta, but wherever Paul went, he tended to witness for Christ. The healings may be God's affirmation that Paul's message is true. Paul likely planted seeds that took root and grew, because eventually Malta became a thriving Christian community. Christian catacombs there reveal the island was largely Christian for some 400 years after the shipwreck. When the travelers leave three months later, the grateful people of Malta honor them and provide them with all the supplies they need.

The Journey to Rome Resumes

At the end of February or early March, the voyagers leave Malta on an Alexandrian vessel that has wintered in the main harbor. They stop in Syracuse, the chief city of Sicily. From there they travel north along the east coast of Sicily to Rhegium, on the southwesternmost tip of Italy. They navigate through the Strait of Messina and are carried by a strong south wind to Puteoli in the western corner of Naples, an area of rugged, volcanic landscape.

When Paul and his companions come ashore, some Christians meet them and invite them to stay an entire week with them in Rome, instead of the three days customary at the time. Roman Christians, hearing of Paul's arrival, gather at the Forum of Appius, a market town 43 miles south of Rome, to meet him. Ten miles farther down the road at Three Taverns, another group joins them. Their presence and fellowship warm Paul's heart and he *"thanked God and took courage"* (28:15).

Paul travels along the Appian Way, which begins at the Forum of Appius and runs northwest straight to the city limits. He passes over the Albanian Mountains, where there is a glorious view of the city and its surroundings. The sight must fill Paul with wonder. No doubt he remembers the letter he wrote to the Christians there. Now many of them meet him at the gates to Rome. As Paul approaches the city, statues of noted Romans appear in ever more frequent numbers. Who could imagine that Paul, a small Jewish man in chains, would make a far greater impact on the world than these immortalized in stone ever would?

Think about how easy it is to support a leader in the midst of his success. Yet the Roman Christians walked miles to welcome a man on his way to trial. The people meeting Paul knew only that he preached Christ and needed their support. Today, too, our leaders need encouragement most when they are having difficulties. How can you support someone in leadership today?

Finally, the centurion hands over the prisoners. The letter from Governor Festus contains little to condemn Paul, and the centurion's testimony about Paul's help during the voyage undoubtedly commends him. Therefore, he is granted permission to live outside the camp with a soldier to guard him at all times.

One Last Chance

Within three days, Paul assembles the leading Jews of the city. (Jews make up about 30,000 of the total Roman population of 600,000.) He explains his imprisonment and assures them he has committed no crime. The Roman Jews say they have heard nothing from Jerusalem regarding Paul, but are curious to know more about Christianity because of negative comments they have heard about the sect.

Later, Paul holds a day-long discussion before a larger audience. He explains, *"It is because of the hope of Israel that I am wearing this chain"* (28:20), and he argues his case by quoting Moses and the prophets. Some are convinced of the truth, but others are not. That a man who was crucified could live again and could be acceptable to God is a scandalous message, because to be hanged on a cross (tree) symbolized being cursed by God (Deuteronomy 21:23, Galatians 3:13). Paul quotes Isaiah 6:9-10, describing the prophet's grief over Israel's refusal to hear and believe God. He uses the passage to indict the Jews in Rome for their failure to accept salvation in Jesus Christ.

The Story Goes On

Early in his first book, Luke described how Jesus preached to the Jews but was rejected and persecuted by them. Now, in the final verses of Acts, he shows how Paul's sermon to the Jews in Rome is met with the same unbelief.

Personalize this lesson.

Again, think about what you learned about the apostle Paul in the latter chapters of this study. What about Paul's *character* stands out to you most? What do you most admire about the way he responded to the challenges He faced? In what way do you most want to be like him?

Bring this desire of your heart before God in prayer. Ask Him to help you grow in this area. Listen as He tells you how to develop the best qualities of His servant Paul.

Dear Esteemed Theophilus, P.S.
Acts 1–28

Memorize God's Word: Philippians 4:6.

❖ The Holy Spirit Comes

1. The Holy Spirit came as promised (2:1-13). What are the immediate evidences of His presence?

   _____

   _____

   _____

2. How is Jesus' promise in 1:8 at least partially fulfilled by these events?

   _____

   _____

3. Throughout the rest of the book of Acts, how do you see Jesus' promise fulfilled in Peter's life?

   _____

   _____

   _____

4. How is it fulfilled in Paul's life?

   _____

   _____

   _____

5. Why do you think the Holy Spirit's power is necessary to be an effective witness?

    _____

    _____

    _____

❖ The Holy Spirit in the Church

6. Read the description of the first church in Acts 2:42-47 and 4:3-35. How do you think the Holy Spirit enabled the new believers to live in such harmony? (See Galatians 5:22-24.)

    _____

    _____

    _____

7. Many Jewish Christians were skeptical that Gentiles could truly be believers. When Cornelius and his household were converted, how did the Holy Spirit show that the Gentiles could have the same faith as the Jews ? (See Acts 10:44-47.)

    _____

    _____

    _____

8. The Holy Spirit also helps to resolve the first major division in the church. What burden did some want to put on the Gentile believers? (See Acts 15:1.)

    _____

    _____

9. In the letter from the Jerusalem Council, how do the apostles express that their decision is the work of the Holy Spirit? (See Acts 15:22-29.)

    _____

    _____

    _____

10. How do you think we can involve the Holy Spirit in church conflicts today?

_____

_____

_____

❖ The Resurrection Is Central

11. According to Paul, what are the central points of the gospel (1 Corinthians 15:1-4)?

_____

_____

12. Why is the Resurrection such a crucial part of our faith (1 Corinthians 15:13-17)?

_____

_____

13. What does the Resurrection mean to you?

_____

_____

_____

❖ The Jews and the Church

14. According to Stephen, what causes the Jews to reject Jesus as their Messiah (Acts 7:51-53)?

_____

_____

15. Do you think these factors still cause people to reject Christ today? Why or why not?

_____

_____

_____

16. How does Paul feel about the Jews? (See Romans 9:3, 10:1.)

_____

_____

17. How does he live his life in order to win them to Christ? (See 1 Corinthians 9:19-23, 10:31-33.)

_____

_____

_____

18. How might you apply this principle in your life?

_____

_____

_____

_____

_____

Apply what you have learned. Think back over all you have learned in this study about being a witness for Christ. (You may want to review some of your answers to the "Apply" sections in previous lessons.) Jot down some of the key lessons. Which one truth do you most want to remember and apply as you share your faith with others? Write out a plan for how you will follow this principle.

Dear Esteemed Theophilus, P.S.
Acts 1–28

Mission Accomplished

You have now finished studying the account of how the gospel traveled from its birthplace in Jerusalem to the capital of the Roman Empire. We trust that the study has been informative, answering some questions and giving new insights. Perhaps it also aroused curiosity, raised new questions, and created a thirst for more research.

Luke probably was not an eyewitness to the incidents recorded in his Gospel, nor the early portion of Acts. His account probably grew from his conversations with many people. He tells of only one reason for writing: to provide Theophilus with an orderly and dependable account of the birth of the church. (Luke's purpose, stated in the prologue of his Gospel, is assumed in Acts.) We do not know for sure why Theophilus was chosen, but it was common practice in that day for people to make their letters available to a much wider audience. For Luke, his account became a way of organizing and presenting his collected material. It begins with Zechariah's vision, where he learned he and his wife, Elizabeth, would become the parents of John the Baptist. Luke's two-volume account closes with Paul's summation in Acts 28:28: *"Therefore let it be known to you that this salvation of God has been sent to the Gentiles; they will listen."*

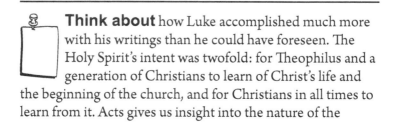

Think about how Luke accomplished much more with his writings than he could have foreseen. The Holy Spirit's intent was twofold: for Theophilus and a generation of Christians to learn of Christ's life and the beginning of the church, and for Christians in all times to learn from it. Acts gives us insight into the nature of the church and practical help in dealing with our problems. We see in Acts a church where even the most strongly held cultural prejudices were abandoned: *"Here there is not Greek and Jew, circumcised and uncircumcised, barbarian, Scythian, slave, free; but Christ is all, and in all"* (Colossians 3:11). What a model for our world!

Luke took different kinds of materials—historical episodes, speeches, conversations between heavenly and earthly beings—and knit them into one narrative without violating literary integrity and continuity. He likely would be the first to admit he was God's instrument in a work of the Holy Spirit.

The Holy Spirit in Acts

Early in his Gospel, Luke highlights the importance of the Holy Spirit in the life of the church. In Luke 3:16, John the Baptist says, *"I baptize you with water, but He who is mightier than I is coming…. He will baptize you with the Holy Spirit and with fire."* In Acts, Luke continues his emphasis on the Spirit's work, showing us how this prophecy was fulfilled (Acts 2:1-4) and how the Spirit directed the spread of the gospel throughout the world.

We see the Spirit working in a variety of ways in Acts. The Spirit struck down Ananias and Sapphira after they lied about the money they gave to the apostles. In the case of Paul's conversion, Ananias of Damascus visits Paul and prays for him to be filled with the Holy Spirit. Ananias was hesitant to visit Paul, who was known for his persecution of Christians. But the Spirit gave Ananias the strength and ability to trust God and follow through with his assignment. God also chose to impart the Holy Spirit to believers in different ways. While Peter was telling Cornelius, his family, and friends—the first Gentile believers to join the church—of Jesus and His forgiveness of sin, *"the Holy Spirit fell on all who heard the word"* (10:44). The Spirit, whose presence was evident by their speaking in tongues and praising God, came on them before either baptism or the laying on of hands.

At Pentecost, Peter assured his audience that the gift of the Spirit was not just for the apostles and their associates. All who accepted Christ would be given the gift (2:38). Later, Paul reminded the Jerusalem Council that

God gives to Gentile believers the same experience of the Holy Spirit He had given to Jewish believers (15:8-9).

Jews and the Church

As Peter and the disciples preached the good news to the Jews, many accepted their message, while others reacted with jealousy and unbelief. Most Jews refused to join the fellowship of the New Testament church, though the original membership was entirely Jewish. Paul never gave up hope of evangelizing his people.

The Resurrection Is Central

The Resurrection, the heart of Christian theology, is a central theme throughout Acts. Without Christ's resurrection, everything the apostles and others had preached would have been false (1 Corinthians 15:14). The Resurrection was of particular importance to Paul, who proclaimed, *"It is with respect to the resurrection of the dead that I am on trial"* (Acts 24:21). Paul would not have met Jesus on the road to Damascus if He had not been raised from the dead.

Rome and the Church

The riots that followed Paul's mission efforts aroused Rome's suspicion of the church, which already had a reputation as a radical group causing chaos and rebellion. Official persecution eventually took many lives.

No official record exists of Paul's last days. His house arrest ended, and according to tradition, he continued to evangelize, perhaps even going to Spain as he had written the Romans he planned to do (Romans 15:23-24). But Nero began his reign of terror against Christians, and Paul was once again taken into custody and jailed in the dungeon of Mamartine Prison at one end of the Roman Forum. One day, the prison doors opened, and Paul was led out to the Appian Way and forced to place his head on the executioner's block. Paul became another martyr whose blood became the seed of the church. At last he was face-to-face with his Lord.

It is fitting that Acts ends abruptly. Truly a work about the acts of the Holy Spirit has no ending. The work begun by Peter at Pentecost—introducing people to Christ—continues today. God calls all of us who know Him to bring the gospel to those around us, and to the ends of the earth.

Personalize this lesson.

 Reflect on the impact this study has had on you. How has it challenged you to grow spiritually? As a result of spending time in Acts, do you want to grow in courage? Perseverance? Passion for sharing your faith? Openness to the Spirit's work in your life? Something else?

Bring your desires before God in prayer, and listen to what He has to say. Thank Him for His work in your life as a result of this study. Ask Him to help you grow in the area He has shown you. Ask Him to use this study to help you become more like Jesus.

Paul's First Missionary Journey

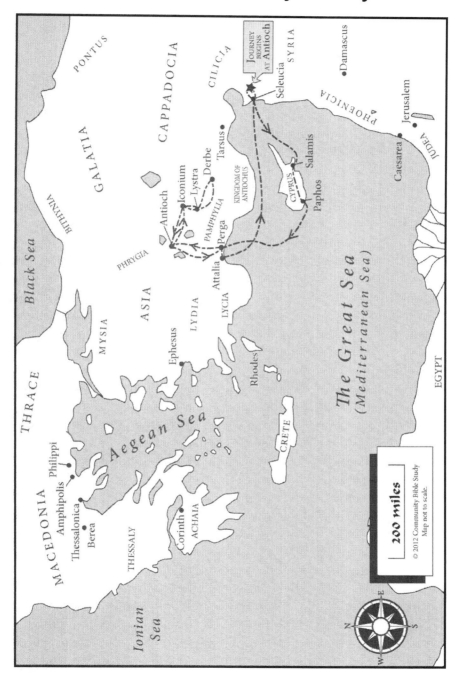

Paul's Second Missionary Journey

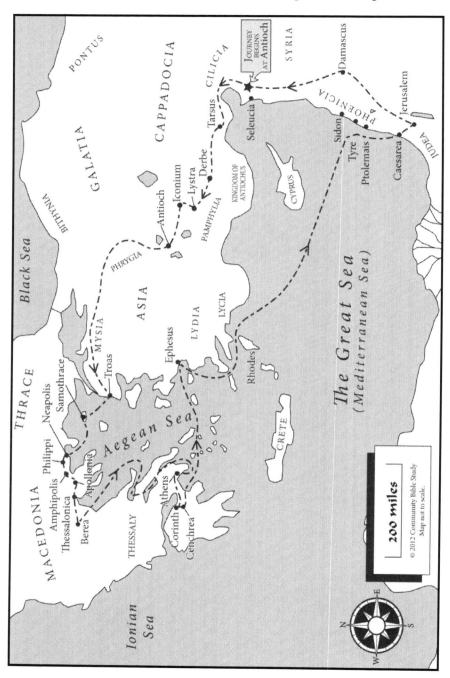

Paul's Third Missionary Journey

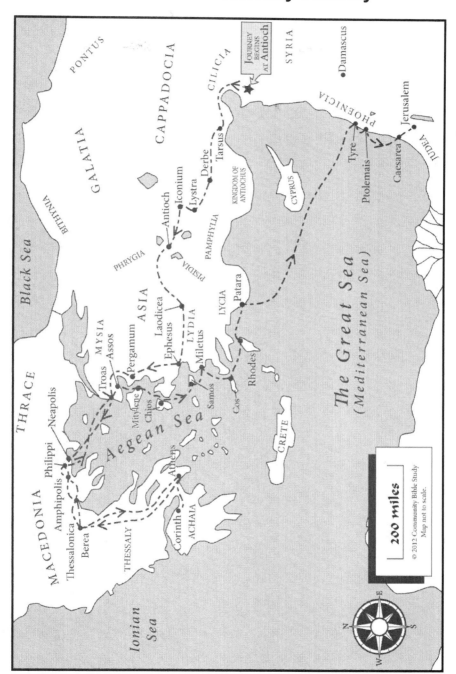

Paul's Journey to Rome

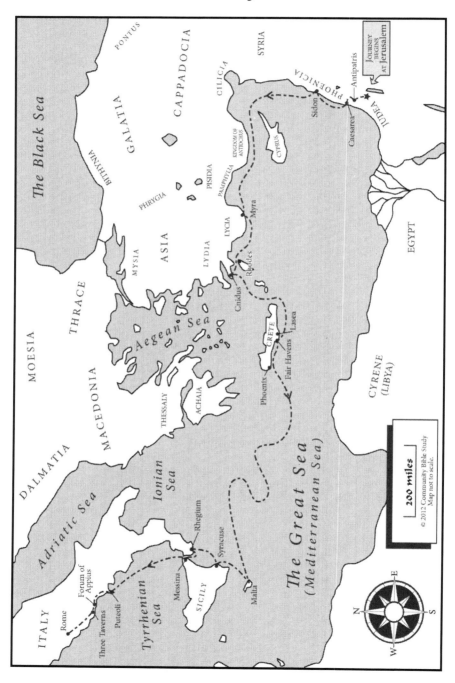

Small Group Leader's Guide

While *Engaging God's Word* is great for personal study, it is generally even more effective and enjoyable when studied with others. Studying with others provides different perspectives and insights, care, prayer support, and fellowship that studying on your own does not. Depending on your personal circumstances, consider studying with your family or spouse, with a friend, in a Sunday school, with a small group at church, work, or in your neighborhood, or in a mentoring relationship.

In a traditional Community Bible Study class, your study would involve a proven four-step method: personal study, a small group discussion facilitated by a trained leader, a lecture covering the passage of Scripture, and a written commentary about the same passage. *Engaging God's Word* provides two of these four steps with the study questions and commentary. When you study with a group, you add another of these— the group discussion. And if you enjoy teaching, you could even provide a modified form of the fourth, the lecture, which in a small group setting might be better termed a wrap-up talk.

Here are some suggestions to help leaders facilitate a successful group study.

1. Decide how long you would like each group meeting to last. For a very basic study, without teaching, time for fellowship, or group prayer, plan on one hour. If you want to allow for fellowship before the meeting starts, add at least 15 minutes. If you plan to give a short teaching, add 15 or 20 minutes. If you also want time for group prayer, add another 10 or 15 minutes. Depending on the components you include for your group, each session will generally last between one and two hours.

2. Set a regular time and place to meet. Meeting in a church classroom or a conference room at work is fine. Meeting in a home is also a good option, and sometimes more relaxed and comfortable.

3. Publicize the study and/or personally invite people to join you.

4. Begin praying for those who have committed to come. Continue to pray for them individually throughout the course of the study.

5. Make sure everyone has his or her own book at least a week before you meet for the first time.

6. Encourage group members to read the first lesson and do the questions before they come to the group meeting.

7. Prepare your own lesson.

8. Prepare your wrap-up talk, if you plan to give one. Here is a simple process for developing a wrap-up talk:

   a. Divide the passage you are studying into two or three divisions. Jot down the verses for each division and describe the content of each with one complete sentence that answers the question, "What is the passage about?"

   b. Decide on the central idea of your wrap-up talk. The central idea is the life-changing principle found in the passage that you believe God wants to implant in the hearts and minds of your group. The central idea answers the question, "What does God want us to learn from this passage?"

   c. Provide one illustration that would make your central idea clear and meaningful to your group. This could be an illustration from your own life, or a story you've read or heard somewhere else.

   d. Suggest one application that would help your group put the central idea into practice.

   e. Choose an aim for your wrap-up talk. The aim answers the question, "What does God want us to do about it?" It encourages specific change in your group's lives, if they choose to respond to the central idea of the passage. Often it takes the form of a question you will ask your group: "Will you, will I choose to … ?"

9. Show up early to the study so you can arrange the room, set up the refreshments (if you are serving any), and welcome people as they arrive.

10. Whether your meeting includes a fellowship time or not, begin the discussion time promptly each week. People appreciate it when you respect their time. Transition into the discussion with prayer, inviting God to guide the discussion time and minister personally to each person present.

11. Model enthusiasm to the group. Let them know how excited you are about what you are learning—and your eagerness to hear what God is teaching them.

12. As you lead through the questions, encourage everyone to participate, but don't force anyone. If one or two people tend to dominate the discussion, encourage quieter ones to participate by saying something like, "Let's hear from someone who hasn't shared yet." Resist the urge to teach during discussion time. This time is for your group to share what they have been discovering.

13. Try to allow time after the questions have been discussed to talk about the "Apply what you have learned," "Think about" and "Personalize this lesson" sections. Encourage your group members in their efforts to partner with God in allowing Him to transform their lives.

14. Transition into the wrap-up talk, if you are doing one (see number 8).

15. Close in prayer. If you have structured your group to allow time for prayer, invite group members to pray for themselves and one another, especially focusing on the areas of growth they would like to see in their lives as a result of their study. If you have not allowed time for group prayer, you as leader can close this time.

16. Before your group finishes their final lesson, start praying and planning for what your next *Engaging God's Word* study will be.

About Community Bible Study

For almost 40 years Community Bible Study has taught the Word of God through in-depth, community-based Bible studies. With nearly 700 classes in the United States as well as classes in more than 70 countries, Community Bible Study purposes to be an "every-person's Bible study, available to all."

Classes for men, women, youth, children, and even babies, are all designed to make members feel loved, cared for, and accepted—regardless of age, ethnicity, socio-economic status, education, or church membership. Because Bible study is most effective in one's heart language, Community Bible Study curriculum has been translated into more than 50 languages.

Community Bible Study makes every effort to stand in the center of the mainstream of historic Christianity, concentrating on the essentials of the Christian faith rather than denominational distinctives. Community Bible Study respects different theological views, preferring to focus on helping people to know God through His Word, grow deeper in their relationships with Jesus, and be transformed into His likeness.

Community Bible Study's focus ... is to glorify God by providing in-depth Bible studies and curriculum in a Christ-centered, grace-filled, and philosophically safe environment.

Community Bible Study's passion ... is the transformation of individuals, families, communities, and generations through the power of God's Word, making disciples of the Lord Jesus Christ.

Community Bible Study's relationship with local churches ... is one of support and respect. Community Bible Study classes are composed of people from many different churches; they are designed to complement and not compete with the ministry of the local church. Recognizing that the Lord has chosen the local church as His primary channel of ministry, Community Bible Study encourages class members to belong to and actively support their local churches and to be servants and leaders in their congregations.

Do you want to experience lasting transformation in your life? Are you ready to go deeper in God's Word? There is probably a Community Bible Study near you! Find out by visiting www.findmyclass.org or scan the QR code on this page.

For more information:

Call   800-826-4181

Email   info@communitybiblestudy.org

Web   www.communitybiblestudy.org

Class   www.findmyclass.org

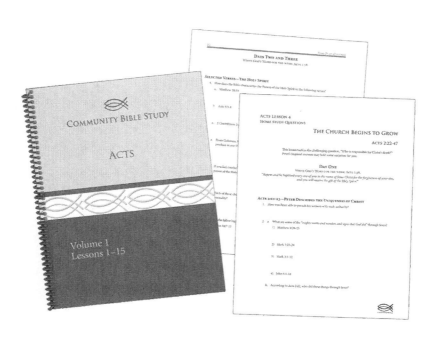

Where will your next Bible study adventure take you?

Engage Bible Studies help you discover the joy and the richness of God's Word and apply it your life.

Check out these titles for your next adventure:

Engaging God's Word: Genesis

Engaging God's Word: Daniel

Engaging God's Word: Job

Engaging God's Word: Mark

Engaging God's Word: Luke

Engaging God's Word: Acts

Engaging God's Word: Romans

Engaging God's Word: Galatians

Engaging God's Word: Ephesians

Engaging God's Word: Philippians

Engaging God's Word: Colossians

Engaging God's Word: 1 & 2 Thessalonians

Engaging God's Word: Hebrews

Engaging God's Word: James

Engaging God's Word: 1 & 2 Peter

Engaging God's Word: Revelation

Also coming soon:

Engage Bible Studies in Spanish!

Available at Amazon.com and in fine bookstores.

Visit engagebiblestudies.com

17033073R00137

Made in the USA
Charleston, SC
23 January 2013